THE NEW
RULES OF GOLF

An official
publication of the
United States
Golf Association

THE NEW RULES OF GOLF

By

TOM WATSON

With Frank Hannigan

RANDOM HOUSE
NEW YORK

Copyright © 1980, 1984 by Random House, Inc.

All rights reserved under International and Pan-Ameri-
can Copyright Conventions. Published in the United
States by Random House, Inc., New York, and simulta-
neously in Canada by Random House of Canada Limited, Toronto. The *1984 Official Rules of Golf* is
published by the United States Golf Association. Copyright © 1984 by United States Golf Association.

Library of Congress Cataloging in Publication Data

Watson, Tom, 1949–
  The new rules of golf.

  Includes index.
  1. Golf—Rules. I. Hannigan, Frank. II. Title.
GV971.W367 1984   796.352′02′022   83-42781
ISBN 0-394-53409-3
ISBN 0-394-72181-0 (pbk.)

Manufactured in the United States of America
  68975

Book design by Dorothy Geiser.

CONTENTS

Playing the Ball

The Putting Green

Ball Moved, Deflected or Stopped

Relief Situations and Procedure

Other Forms of Play

Administration

INTRODUCTION

The Rules of Golf are the joint responsibility of two organizations—the Royal and Ancient Golf Club of St. Andrews, Scotland (R&A) and the United States Golf Association (USGA). They jointly write and interpret the Rules, and every national golf organization, professional and amateur, defers to their judgment. An agreement exists to the effect that neither the USGA nor the R&A will act unilaterally and that amendments will be adopted only every fourth year. This book is published as the 1984 changes take effect.

During 1980 the R&A and USGA embarked on a four-year project to recodify the Rules of Golf. They reorganized the Rules into a more logical order, changed the captions to make them more helpful and rewrote much of the language to conform to common usage.

They purposefully introduced some repetition, but for the good cause of making it easier to find in one place everything needed to answer a question. And they also incorporated some of the more important interpretations (known as Decisions) into the Rules themselves.

At the same time they attempted to simplify the substance of the Rules where feasible. Their purpose was to make the Rules easier to learn and use for officials, serious competitors and the average golfer who wants to play by the Rules.

This book contains the end product. It represents the first thorough overhaul of the Rules since the last recodification in 1951. The principal changes are summarized briefly on pages 166–168.

This book, like its predecessor, is not aimed at any one segment of golfers. It assumes a basic understanding of golf terminology, but beginners as well as experienced players can profit from the experience.

My point of view remains unashamedly traditional. There exists only one set of Rules and here they are. "Winter Rules," which permit the golfer to improve the lie by moving the ball, should be shunned except when it is otherwise impossible to play.

The great satisfaction of golf comes from accepting, meeting and overcoming the challenge of a singularly difficult game. Relaxing the

Rules in order to make the game easier would diminish the joy that follows a great round.

That isn't to say that I think the Rules are perfect. They are man-made, and they deal with a very complicated game played on a vast and irregular playing field, so perfection isn't possible. What is perfect, though, is that the playing Rules are the same for everyone in the more than sixty nations where golf is played. That doesn't happen in other games.

Throughout this book are references to Decisions—formal and published clarifications of the Rules. Prior to 1984, the USGA and R&A each had its own set of Decisions. As part of the reorganization project, however, both sets of Decisions were consolidated and now are available in one volume—a massive, but eminently worthwhile, undertaking.

This is the second version of this book. The first, published four years earlier, became—to my astonishment and pleasure—one of the most popular books ever published about golf.

My thanks again are extended to C.A. (Tony) Wimpfheimer of Random House, who proposed that there be such a book.

Among the many who read the manuscript and offered helpful suggestions was William J. Williams, Jr., chairman of the USGA Rules of Golf Committee.

The manuscript was thoroughly examined and improved by P. J. Boatwright, Jr., USGA Executive Director of Rules and Competitions, who is an extraordinary authority on the subject. Others in the USGA family who provided help were Tom Meeks, C. McDonald England and Dr. Richard Silver.

ETIQUETTE

Courtesy on the Course

Consideration for Other Players

The player who has the honor should be allowed to play before his opponent or fellow-competitor tees his ball.

No one should move, talk or stand close to or directly behind the ball or the hole when a player is addressing the ball or making a stroke.

In the interest of all, players should play without delay.

No player should play until the players in front are out of range.

Players searching for a ball should signal the players behind them to pass as soon as it becomes apparent that the ball will not easily be found. They should not search for five minutes before doing so. They should not continue play until the players following them have passed and are out of range.

When the play of a hole has been completed, players should immediately leave the putting green.

Priority on the Course

In the absence of special rules, two-ball matches should have precedence over and be entitled to pass any three- or four-ball match.

A single player has no standing and should give way to a match of any kind.

Any match playing a whole round is entitled to pass a match playing a shorter round.

If a match fails to keep its place on the course and loses more than one clear hole on the players in front, it should allow the match following to pass.

Care of the Course

Holes in Bunkers

Before leaving a bunker, a player should carefully fill up and smooth over all holes and footprints made by him.

Replace Divots; Repair Ball Marks and Damage by Spikes

Through the green, a player should ensure that any turf cut or displaced by him is replaced at once and pressed down and that any damage to the putting green made by a ball is carefully repaired. Damage to the putting green caused by golf shoe spikes should be repaired *on completion of the hole.*

Damage to Greens—Flagsticks, Bags, etc.

Players should ensure that, when putting down bags or the flagstick, no damage is done to the putting green and that neither they nor their caddies damage the hole by standing close to it, in handling the flagstick or in removing the ball from the hole. The flagstick should be properly replaced in the hole before the players leave the putting green. Players should not damage the putting green by leaning on their putters, particularly when removing the ball from the hole.

Golf Carts

Local notices regulating the movement of golf carts should be strictly observed.

Damage Through Practice Swings

In taking practice swings, players should avoid causing damage to the course, particularly the tees, by removing divots.

Etiquette involves the rules of conduct which ought to guide golfers in their relationships with one another and with the course. Ours is a sensitive, perhaps even a fragile, game. If it is to prosper or be fun to play (which may be the highest form of prosperity), golfers have to behave decently. The game could not survive public displays of temper or acts of recrimination against a tee or putting green.

The relationship between the golfer and the course is fascinating. I can't think of another sport in which the playing arena must be maintained, in part, by the players. In golf we take it for granted that the player has the responsibility for performing the elementary housekeeping chores of replacing divots, repairing ball marks and smoothing bunkers.

There is, however, a provision of the Etiquette section which is often ignored, or so it seems to me. That's the one that reads: "In the interest of all, players should play without delay."

Slow play has long been golf's disease. Four players in the same group should never need more than four hours to play 18 holes of golf. The five-hour round is a horror, and it says much for the appeal of the game that, hating the prospect though they must, golfers go right on playing.

I don't think there's any correlation between scores and pace of play. It's not necessary to agonize over shots in order to shoot sub-par scores. At the same time, the high-handicap player has no excuse for dawdling. I have friends who can't break 100, but we can play together without feeling that we're holding one another up.

I have a reputation for being one of the fastest players on the pro tour. I began to play golf with my father when I was eight years old and with the clear-cut understanding that I was more than welcome, provided I kept up. So I became a fast player at a very early age.

DEFINITIONS

DEFINITIONS

Experienced readers of the Rules of Golf will notice that the presentation of the Definitions has been fundamentally changed in 1984. The alterations are:

- The Definitions have been regrouped so as to be strictly in alphabetical order. For example, the Definition of "wrong ball" used to be mysteriously buried in the same unit with "Ball in Play" and "Provisional Ball." Now you can find "wrong ball" where it should be—as the last Definition.

- The numbers have been eliminated.

- The Definitions are repeated, when applicable, as introductions to the Rules themselves. Now a golfer who wonders if he's entitled to free relief from a boundary fence and instinctively heads for Rule 24 covering obstructions and what to do about them will find not only the relief procedure but also the very Definition of an obstruction. And no, a boundary fence is not an obstruction.

The Definitions are basic. They exist because many key words and special terms in the Rules are not those we use in everyday language and must therefore be clarified.

Golfers tend to resort to the Rules only when they have a problem and are in a hurry for an answer. They'll run into a phrase such as "through the green" and the mind tends to boggle. It doesn't help, of course, that "through the green" is often misused by television commentators to apply to balls hit *beyond* the green, when it means something entirely different.

The Definitions follow, punctuated by occasional comments which are inserted for the purpose of, if you'll pardon the expression, defining the Definitions.

Addressing the Ball

A player has "addressed the ball" when he has taken his *stance* and has also grounded his club, except that in a *hazard,* a player has addressed the ball when he has taken his stance.

Advice

"Advice" is any counsel or suggestion which could influence a player in determining his play, the choice of a club or the method of making a *stroke*.

Don't Always Address a Ball

If a ball is on a slope, or perched on high grass, anywhere outside a hazard, it makes sense to play the next stroke without addressing the ball, because if the ball moves after address, the player is deemed to have caused it to move and incurs a penalty stroke. Note that I have not addressed the ball because the club has not been grounded. If the ball moves, and I haven't caused it to move, there is no penalty and I would play the ball from where it then lies. This advice doesn't apply within a hazard, where the act of address is completed as soon as the stance is taken. (R. 18)

> Information on the Rules or on matters of public information, such as the position of hazards or the flagstick on the putting green, is not advice.

The second paragraph says you're not asking for "advice" when you say "Where's the hole?" When the answer comes back "It's in the back of the green," that's not giving "advice" either.

See "Move or Moved."

See "Holed."

See "Lost Ball."

Ball Deemed to Move

Ball Holed

Ball Lost

Ball in Play

A ball is "in play" as soon as the player has made a *stroke* on the *teeing ground.* It remains in play until holed out, except when it is *out of bounds, lost* or lifted, or another ball has been substituted under an applicable Rule; a ball so substituted becomes the ball in play.

There can only be one ball "in play" for one player at one time. If a player's ball heads in the direction of a water hazard and the player drops and plays another ball, the second ball is then "in play." If the player then finds the original ball to be playable and plays it, he has played a "wrong ball."

Bunker

A "bunker" is a *hazard* consisting of a prepared area of ground, often a hollow, from which turf or soil has been removed and replaced with sand or the like. Grass-covered ground bordering or within the bunker is not part of the bunker.

If you insist on calling it a "sand trap," you've fallen into the trap of substituting common usage for common sense. The phrase "sand trap" does not occur in the Rules.

Caddie

A "caddie" is one who carries or handles a player's clubs during play and otherwise assists him in accordance with the Rules.

When one caddie is employed by more than one player, he is always deemed to be the caddie of the player whose ball is involved, and *equipment* carried by him is deemed to be that player's equipment, except when the caddie acts upon specific directions of another player, in which case he is considered to be that other player's caddie.

Casual Water

"Casual water" is any temporary accumulation of water on the *course* which is visible before or after the player takes his *stance* and is not in a *water hazard.* Snow and ice are either casual water or *loose impediments,* at the option of the player. Dew is not casual water.

The disclaimer about dew is a useful little addition in the 1984 Rules. Also note that soft, mushy ground, or mud, does not qualify as casual water.

Committee

The "Committee" is the committee in charge of the competition or, if the matter does not arise in a competition, the committee in charge of the *course.*

In everyday play the Committee is not likely to be available. The golf professional is usually authorized to act on behalf of the Committee.

Competitor

A "competitor" is a player in a stroke competition. A "fellow-competitor" is any person with whom the competitor plays. Neither is *partner* of the other.

In stroke play foursome and four-ball competitions, where the context so admits, the word "competitor" or "fellow-competitor" shall be held to include his partner.

"Competitor" is a nice old-fashioned and useful word which, like "bunker," doesn't get the respect it deserves. The people with whom you are playing in stroke play are "fellow-competitors." Calling them "playing partners" is inaccurate and can lead to misunderstandings, since the word "partner" suggests someone with whom you are in business and whom you can assist.

The "course" is the whole area within which play is permitted. See Rule 33-2.

Course

"Equipment" is anything used, worn or carried by or for the player except any ball he has played and any small object, such as a coin or a tee, when used to mark the position of a ball or the extent of an area in which a ball is to be dropped. Equipment includes a golf cart, whether or not motorized. If such a cart is shared by more than one player, its status under the Rules is the same as that of a caddie employed by more than one player. See "Caddie."

Equipment

Golf carts are tough on the Rules, just as they are on the turf of our courses. The problems that stem from a cart deflecting or moving a ball are myriad. They are, however, resolved in two Decisions. Here they are:

Ball Moved by Golf Cart Shared by Two Players

"Under the Definition of 'Equipment,' equipment includes a golf cart, whether or not motorized. If two players share a golf cart, the cart and everything in it are, for purposes of applying the Rules, deemed to be the equipment of the player whose ball is involved, except that, when the cart is being driven or pulled by one of the players, the cart and everything in it is considered to be that player's equipment.

"Thus, for example, in a singles match, if A and B are sharing a cart and the cart moves A's ball which was at rest, A would be penalized one stroke if he was driving or pulling the cart (Rule 18-2a). B would be penalized one stroke if he was driving or pulling the cart (Rule 18-3b), unless the incident occurred during search (Rule 18-3a)."

Ball Deflected or Stopped by Golf Cart Shared by Two Players

". . . In a singles match, if A and B are sharing a cart and A's ball in motion is deflected or stopped by the cart, A loses the hole (Rule 19-2a) unless the cart is being driven or pulled by B when the incident occurs. If B is driving or pulling the cart, there is no penalty, and A would have the option of playing his ball as it lies or replaying the stroke (Rule 19-3b).

"In terms of this Decision, a golf cart is not 'being driven or pulled' when it is stationary or unoccupied; in such circumstances, therefore, it is deemed to be the equipment of the player whose ball is involved."

9

Fellow-Competitor | See "Competitor."

Flagstick | The "flagstick" is a movable straight indicator, with or without bunting or other material attached, centered in the hole to show its position. It shall be circular in cross-section.

Forecaddie | A "forecaddie" is one who is employed by the Committee to indicate to players the position of balls on the course, and is an *outside agency*.

Ground Under Repair | "Ground under repair" is any portion of the *course* so marked by order of the Committee or so declared by its authorized representative. It includes material piled for removal and a hole made by a greenkeeper, even if not so marked. Stakes and lines defining ground under repair are in such ground.

Note 1: Grass cuttings and other material left on the course which have been abandoned and are not intended to be removed are not ground under repair unless so marked.

Note 2: The Committee may make a Local Rule prohibiting play from ground under repair.

Ground under repair is customarily and best defined by white lines. When a ball touches the white line it is considered in ground under repair and the relief offered in Rule 25 can be obtained.

Why would a Committee want to make a Local Rule prohibiting play from ground under repair, as contemplated in Note 2? Because some areas—recently seeded or sodded—need protection.

A couple of interpretations clarifying ground under repair:

● Is a rut or a groove made by a maintenance vehicle considered a hole made by a greenkeeper?

When Is a Ball in Ground Under Repair?

This ball is in an area marked ground under repair because it touches the line. I'd be entitled to take relief even if the ball was outside the area, but my stance caused me to stand on the line or within the marked ground.
(R. 25)

Grass in a Bunker
The Rules allow you to ground your club in a bunker in a grassy area within the bunker. Grass-covered ground within a bunker is not considered part of the hazard.

Answer: No, but a player whose ball is in a deep rut would be justified in asking the Committee to declare the rut to be ground under repair, and the Committee would be justified in doing so.

● What's the status of a tree stump?

Answer: There is no free relief from a tree stump not marked as ground under repair unless it is in the process of being unearthed or cut up, in which case it is "material piled for removal" and thus ground under repair.

A "hazard" is any *bunker* or *water hazard.*	**Hazards**
The "hole" shall be 4¼ inches (108 mm) in diameter and at least 4 inches (100 mm) deep. If a lining is used, it shall be sunk at least 1 inch (25 mm) below the *putting green* surface unless the nature of the soil makes it impracticable to do so; its outer diameter shall not exceed 4¼ inches (108 mm).	**Hole**

The parenthetical use of millimeters is a historic first concession to the metric system in the Rules.

A ball is "holed" when it is at rest within the circumference of the hole and all of it is below the level of the lip of the hole.	**Holed**
The side entitled to play first from the *teeing ground* is said to have the "honor."	**Honor**
A "lateral water hazard" is a *water hazard* or that part of a water hazard so situated that it is not possible or is deemed by the Committee to be impracticable to drop a ball behind	**Lateral Water Hazard**

11

the water hazard and keep the spot at which the ball last crossed the margin of the water hazard between the player and the hole.

That part of a water hazard to be played as a lateral water hazard should be distinctively marked.

Note: *Lateral water hazards should be defined by red stakes or lines.*

The problem with understanding this definition is that a "lateral water hazard" does not necessarily have to run lateral, or parallel, to the line of play. It's up to the Committee to make the distinction, and the Committee should be guided by the principle of whether or not it's fair or practicable to drop behind the hazard and keep the spot at which the ball last crossed the margin between the player and the hole. If not, the hazard should be categorized as "lateral" so that the player can avail himself of the extra options expressed in Rule 26-1c.

Loose Impediments

"Loose impediments" are natural objects such as stones, leaves, twigs, branches and the like, dung, worms and insects and casts or heaps made by them, provided they are not fixed or growing, are not solidly embedded and do not adhere to the ball.

Sand and loose soil are loose impediments on the *putting green* but not elsewhere.

Snow and ice are either *casual water* or loose impediments, at the option of the player.

Dew is not a loose impediment.

A query lodged with the USGA led to one of the classic Decisions. Is a half-eaten pear in front of a ball in a bunker considered a natural object or an artificial object? If it's natural (and therefore a loose

Sand Can't Always be Removed

Sand has been splashed from a bunker onto both the putting green and the apron just off the green. Both areas are on my line to the hole and might affect the roll. Nevertheless, the sand off the green is not *a loose impediment and may not be moved; the sand on the green is a loose impediment and may be removed. (R. 23)*

impediment), it can't be moved; if it's artificial (and thus an "obstruction"), it can be removed without penalty under Rule 24. The bunker in which the pear was lodged was not in close proximity to a pear tree.

Answer: If the player removed the pear, she violated Rule 13-4, the penalty for which is: Match play—Loss of hole; Stroke play—Two strokes.

A pear is a natural object (an obstruction must be artificial). When detached from a tree it is a loose impediment. The facts that a pear has been half-eaten and there is no pear tree in the vicinity do not alter the status of the pear.

Loose impediments may be transformed into obstructions through processes of construction or manufacturing. For example, a log (loose impediment) that has been split and has had legs attached to it has been changed by construction into a bench (obstruction); or a piece of coal (loose impediment) is considered an obstruction when manufactured into a charcoal briquet.

Lost Ball

A ball is "lost" if
a. It is not found or identified as his by the player within five minutes after the player's side or his or their caddies have begun to search for it; or
b. The player has put another ball into play under the Rules, even though he may not have searched for the original ball; or
c. The player has played any stroke with a *provisional ball* from the place where the original ball is likely to be or from a point nearer the hole than that place, whereupon the provisional ball becomes the *ball in play.*
Time spent in playing a *wrong ball* is not counted in the five-minute period allowed for search.

Here's what some key Decisions on the subject of lost balls say:
• A player searches for his ball for two minutes after hitting a wild fairway wood shot, declares his ball is lost and heads back toward the original spot. Before he drops another ball and within the five-minute search period, his caddie finds his first ball.

Answer: As the player had not put another ball in play under the Rules, he could play the first ball.
• What happens in stroke play when a player searches for a ball for less than five minutes, gives up the search, returns to the tee and plays another ball? Then the original ball is found, the player picks up the second ball and he plays the first.

Answer: The original was lost when the player put the second ball in play—no matter how long the search. When he lifted the second ball he violated Rule 18-2 (one-stroke penalty). When he played a stroke with the original ball he played a wrong ball (two strokes under Rule 15-3). Finally, if he doesn't rectify the mistake by replacing and playing the second ball before he plays from the next tee, he's disqualified.
• Jimmy Thomson, reputedly the longest hitter in the world during the 1930s, asked how to rule when two players are playing identical

balls, i.e., balls of the same brand and marking and with the same numbers. The balls come to rest very close together, and the players are not sure of the ownership of either.

Answer: It may seem harsh, but both balls are to be treated as lost, since neither player can identify one as his. A pencil mark or a dot made by a marking pen in a dimple is all it takes to identify a ball properly.

● On a par-3 hole, in a stroke play event, a player hit wildly and, thinking his original might be lost, played a provisional ball. The result with the provisional ball was excellent. In fact, it came to rest one inch from the hole. Must the player search for the original ball?

Answer: No. He can tap the ball near the hole in for a 4.

● An incident on the tour involving Miller Barber led to these two:

A player is reasonably certain that his ball is high up in a tree but he can't see it and therefore can't identify it. Answer: The ball is lost.

A player can see a ball in a tree but can't retrieve it to identify it as his. Answer: The ball is lost, which means the player is not allowed to treat it as unplayable; he must suffer the stroke-and-distance penalty. (That actually happened to me on the 18th hole at Cypress Point in the 1983 Crosby Tournament. I could see a ball, which was probably mine, high up in a tree, but since I couldn't identify it as mine I had to go back to the tee instead of declaring it unplayable and dropping it near the base of the tree.)

Marker

A "marker" is one who is appointed by the Committee to record a *competitor's* score in stroke play. He may be a *fellow-competitor*. He is not a *referee*.

A marker should not lift a ball or mark its position unless authorized to do so by the competitor and, unless he is a fellow-competitor, should not attend the flagstick or stand at the hole or mark its position.

The marker in stroke play today is invariably a fellow-competitor. On the PGA Tour you may have noticed someone, usually in a uniform, walking with each group of players and recording scores. Her function is to report the scores at the end of each hole to a telephone operator. The scores she reports are the source material for television and scoreboards, but they are not official.

There's no such thing as a marker in match play. Keeping a hole-by-hole card in match play is a useful way of tracking the match, but the card has no official status.

Matches

See "Sides and Matches."

Move or Moved

A ball is deemed to have "moved" if it leaves its position and comes to rest in any other place.

A ball has not moved if it only jiggles or oscillates.

Observer

An "observer" is one who is appointed by the Committee to assist a *referee* to decide questions of fact and to report to

No Relief from Boundary Fence or Stakes

Even though they are artificial objects, out-of-bounds fences and their posts are not obstructions. Moreover, boundary fences, posts and stakes are regarded as "things fixed" and may not be moved. In this situation, I don't have any choice but to declare the ball unplayable and accept a penalty stroke. (R. 24)

him any breach of a Rule. An observer should not attend the flagstick, stand at or mark the position of the hole, or lift the ball or mark its position.

Obstructions

An "obstruction" is anything artificial, including the artificial surfaces and sides of roads and paths, except:

a. Objects defining *out of bounds,* such as walls, fences, stakes and railings;

b. Any part of an immovable artificial object which is out of bounds; and

c. Any construction declared by the Committee to be an integral part of the course.

This definition has been simplified by eliminating the old and complicated reference to "artificially surfaced banks or beds" within water hazards. But the payoff occurs within Rule 24, where it's written that there is no longer any relief from *immovable* obstructions if the ball lies in a water hazard.

The Committee has the latitude to preserve the character of a hole which might be lost if free relief was given from something artificial on that hole. The artificial construction is then classified as "an integral part of the course." The best-known case occurs on the 17th hole —the Road Hole—of the Old Course at St. Andrews in Scotland. When you miss the green to the right, the ball invariably winds up on the blacktop road adjacent to and well below the green. When I'm on the road, I pray to get down in three. The road makes the 17th hole at St. Andrews one of the great par-4 holes anywhere.

Out of Bounds

"Out of bounds" is ground on which play is prohibited. When out of bounds is defined by reference to stakes or a fence or as being beyond stakes or a fence, the out of bounds line is determined by the nearest inside points of the stakes or fence posts at ground level excluding angled supports.

When out of bounds is defined by a line on the ground, the line itself is out of bounds.

The out of bounds line is deemed to extend vertically upwards and downwards.

A ball is out of bounds when all of it lies out of bounds.

A player may stand out of bounds to play a ball lying within bounds.

Outside Agency

An "outside agency" is any agency not part of the match, or, in stroke play, not part of a competitor's side, and includes a referee, a marker, an observer or a forecaddie. Neither wind nor water is an outside agency.

Golf balls are occasionally deflected or moved by alien objects and beings such as dogs, spectators and trash containers. Those are called "outside agencies," and within the body of the Rules you'll find what to do, depending on the circumstances, when an outside agency intrudes.

16

In Bounds and Out of Bounds

The out-of-bounds line is determined by the inside points of fence posts at ground level. A ball is out of bounds only when all of it lies out of bounds. Rules of Golf officials sometimes decide close calls by stretching a string from post to post. The ball at the bottom is in bounds; the ball at left is out of bounds. (R. 27)

17

Partner   A "partner" is a player associated with another player on the same side.

In a threesome, foursome or a four-ball match where the context so admits, the word "player" shall be held to include his partner.

Penalty Stroke   A "penalty stroke" is one added to the score of a player or *side* under certain Rules. In a threesome or foursome, penalty strokes do not affect the order of play.

Provisional Ball   A "provisional ball" is a ball played under Rule 27-2 for a ball which may be *lost* outside a *water hazard* or may be *out of bounds*. It ceases to be a provisional ball when the Rule provides either that the player continue play with it as the *ball in play* or that it be abandoned.

The phrase "provisional ball" is often confused with "second ball" in Rule 3-3. The former is a ball you may play in order to save time when your ball may be lost (not in a water hazard) or out of bounds, but you're not sure; the latter is a ball you are allowed to play in stroke play when you are doubtful of your rights or the proper procedure.

Key point: You may not play a provisional ball for the reason that the ball may be lost in a water hazard.

Putting Green   The "putting green" is all ground of the hole being played which is specially prepared for putting or otherwise defined as such by the Committee. A ball is on the putting green when any part of it touches the putting green.

An "apron" or "collar" (words that do not appear in the Rules) is a narrow strip cut nearly as low as the green but not considered part of the putting green.

Referee   A "referee" is one who is appointed by the Committee to accompany players to decide questions of fact and apply the Rules of Golf. He shall act on any breach of a Rule which he observes or is reported to him.

A referee should not attend the flagstick, stand at or mark the position of the hole, or lift the ball or mark its position.

Very few golfers ever have the opportunity to play with a referee accompanying them. It's too bad, because the presence of a referee seems to put the game on a slightly higher plane. Referees can enhance the final matches of club championships, provided they're competent. The USGA offers a fascinating booklet for the bargain price of 50¢ on the subject called "Duties of Officials Under the Rules of Golf." (Write to the USGA, Far Hills, NJ 07931.)

Rub of the Green   A "rub of the green" occurs when a ball in motion is accidentally deflected or stopped by any *outside agency* (see Rule 19-1).

The term "Rule" includes Local Rules made by the Committee under Rule 33-8a.

SIDE: A player, or two or more players who are *partners*.

SINGLE: A match in which one plays against another.

THREESOME: A match in which one plays against two, and each side plays one ball.

FOURSOME: A match in which two play against two, and each side plays one ball.

THREE-BALL: A match in which three play against one another, each playing his own ball.

BEST-BALL: A match in which one plays against the better ball of two or the best ball of three players.

FOUR-BALL: A match in which two play their better ball against the better ball of two other players.

I'm a traditionalist and am therefore among the minority in the United States who believe we should cling to the proper usage of the terms in this Definition and fight the good, if losing, fight against the bastardization of these terms. Thus:

• A threesome is not three who are playing together; it's a form of competition that is virtually extinct. ("Twosome" is an ugly word often, and mistakenly, applied to two players paired in stroke play.)

• A foursome is a fascinating kind of competition in which partners play alternating strokes. It is not four players who are playing together. This form of play is sometimes and unnecessarily referred to as a "Scotch Foursome."

• A four-ball is by far the most popular form of golf played in this country. Alas, too often it's called a "best-ball," which, again, is an interesting but out-of-vogue kind of match covered in Rule 30.

Taking the "stance" consists in a player placing his feet in position for and preparatory to making a *stroke*.

The "stipulated round" consists of playing the holes of the course in their correct sequence unless otherwise authorized by the Committee. The number of holes in a stipulated round is 18 unless a smaller number is authorized by the Committee. As to extension of stipulated round in match play, see Rule 2-4.

This gives us an excuse to paraphrase a celebrated Stipulated Round question and answer.

• In match play, two players were so busy talking that they failed to play two holes. They did not realize the omission until the results of the match were posted and they wondered why their scores were so good. It was too late in the day to send them out again to play the whole 18, and to wait until the following day to replay their match would have delayed the whole flight and upset the tournament schedule. We sent them out immediately after their error was discovered to play the two holes they had left out, and we are anxious to know whether or not this was correct. Unfortunately, those two holes

The Teeing Ground

The teeing ground is a rectangular area two club-lengths in depth. You can tee your ball anywhere in that rectangle. You're not required to stand within it. I've chosen to stand outside the teeing ground in the bottom picture because I feel that setup makes it easier to stay out of the trouble that lurks on the left side of the hole.

changed the result of the match, and there has been considerable discussion as to whether our ruling was legal.

What is the correct ruling in such a case?

Answer: The Committee's decision is final (see Rule 34-3). However, the Committee should *not* have directed that the two omitted holes be played belatedly. The result of the match should have been allowed to stand as originally posted—see Rule 2-5. Had the players agreed to play less than the stipulated round, both would have been subject to disqualification—see Rule 1-3.

Stroke

A "stroke" is the forward movement of the club made with the intention of fairly striking at and moving the ball.

The key words are "forward" and "intention." Here's what some Decisions say about strokes:

• A player begins the forward movement of the club with the intention of hitting the ball but stops his swing before he has progressed halfway.

Answer: Since the player's intention to move the ball died before he was able to move it, there was no stroke.

• A Canadian asked for confirmation of a club ruling he'd made (correctly): In a mixed foursome competition, it was the woman's turn to play a stroke requiring a long carry over water. Her partner counseled her to "whiff" the ball, promising to put the ball on the green with his next stroke. The woman's "whiff" was not a stroke, since she did not intend to strike the ball. Her partner therefore played out of turn.

Teeing Ground

The "teeing ground" is the starting place for the hole to be played. It is a rectangular area two club-lengths in depth, the front and sides of which are defined by the outside limits of two tee-markers. A ball is outside the teeing ground when all of it lies outside the teeing ground.

This is the first time we run into a reference to "club-lengths," which occurs time and again within the Rules proper. The term is used instead of a specific distance, such as "six feet," because golfers aren't expected to carry tape measures. Any club is acceptable and, obviously, a driver is the best candidate, since it will make for the biggest rectangular area.

Through the Green

"Through the green" is the whole area of the *course* except:

a. The *teeing ground* and *putting green* of the hole being played; and

b. All *hazards* on the course.

The important phrase "through the green" recurs throughout the Rules. It's a phrase that encompasses most of the course but not the tee of the hole being played or the putting green of the hole being played or any hazard. Everything else is "through the green." The distinctions are often critical. For example, if your ball is just off the green and there's casual water between your ball and the hole, you get no relief—that is, you don't get to move it, since the ball is "through the green." But if the ball is on the putting green in the same circumstance, a special kind of relief is available under Rule 25-1.

Water Hazard

A "water hazard" is any sea, lake, pond, river, ditch, surface drainage ditch or other open water course (whether or not containing water) and anything of a similar nature.

All ground or water within the margin of a water hazard is part of the water hazard. The margin of a water hazard is deemed to extend vertically upwards. Stakes and lines defining the margins of water hazards are in the hazards.

Note: *Water hazards (other than* lateral *water hazards) should be defined by yellow stakes or lines.*

Stakes used to define hazards are obstructions and may be removed when they interfere, but as the Definition of "out of bounds" reveals, stakes defining boundaries may not be moved.

There is some understandable confusion about the proper names for and distinctions between types of water hazards. Think of it this way: there are only two kinds. The most common is, quite simply, a "water hazard," and is often called a "regular water hazard." The other is a "lateral water hazard."

Wrong Ball

A "wrong ball" is any ball other than:
a. The *ball in play.*
b. A *provisional ball* or
c. In stroke play, a second ball played under Rule 3-3 or Rule 20-7b.

THE
RULES
OF PLAY

THE GAME

RULE 1

THE GAME

1-1
General

The Game of Golf consists in playing a ball from the <u>teeing ground</u> into the hole by a <u>stroke</u> or successive strokes in accordance with the Rules.

PENALTY FOR BREACH OF RULE 1-1:
Match play—Loss of hole; Stroke play—Disqualification.

1-2
Exerting Influence on Ball

No player or caddie shall take any action to influence the position or the movement of a ball except in accordance with the Rules.

PENALTY FOR BREACH OF RULE 1-2:
Match play—Loss of hole; Stroke play—Two strokes.
Note: *In the case of a serious breach of Rule 1-2, the Committee may impose a penalty of disqualification.*

1-3
Agreement to Waive Rules

Players shall not agree to exclude the operation of any Rule or to waive any penalty incurred.

PENALTY FOR BREACH OF RULE 1-3:
*Match play—Disqualification of both sides; Stroke play—
Disqualification of competitors concerned.*

1-4
Points Not Covered by Rules

If any point in dispute is not covered by the Rules, the decision shall be made in accordance with equity.

1-1. General
   The Rules of Golf begin with a straightforward definition of the game itself. One sentence of twenty-seven words does the job.
   This is the place you should begin to pick out the key words and

24

phrases used in the Definitions and to familiarize yourself with the precise language used throughout the Rules. There are no fewer than five checkpoints in this sentence of twenty-seven words:

- "Playing *a* ball" means playing *one* ball. You may not change to a shiny new ball once you've cleared a water hazard or landed safely on a putting green.
- "The 'teeing ground,' " according to the Definition, "is the starting place for the hole to be played," and its dimensions are specific.
- "Into the hole" reveals that, in stroke play, if you fail to hole out, you have failed to play the game—and that you're disqualified.
- "By successive strokes" calls for an understanding of a stroke, which according to the Definition "is the forward movement of the club made with the intention of fairly striking at and moving the ball." Incidentally, Richard Peters came to play in the very first U.S. Amateur Championship in 1895 intending to putt with a billiard cue. There is no such thing as a stroke made with a billiard cue, because a billiard cue isn't a club.
- "In accordance with the Rules" is what this book is about. In order to understand and enjoy the game you *must* know the Rules.

1-2. Exerting Influence on Ball

Some examples illustrating what Rule 1-2 means (taking "any action to influence the position or the movement of a ball") are found in Decisions.

- A player purposely steps on and damages (or improves) his opponent's line of putt. Violation!
- A player in a professional event in Wales ingeniously placed his bag parallel to the line of a short putt to shield the line from the wind. Violation!
- In the California Amateur Championship at stroke play a competitor who had holed out repaired spike marks on the line of putt of a fellow-competitor. Violation! The player who did the repair job is penalized two strokes. If the player whose line was improved sanctioned the repair job, he too should be penalized two strokes, but under Rule 13-2. If it's found that there was an agreement between the two to repair damage on each other's line of putt, both should be disqualified under Rule 1-3 for having agreed to waive a Rule.
- A player's putt hangs on the lip of the hole. He jumps as high as he can, three feet from the cup. The ball falls in. Violation!

1-3. Agreement to Waive Rules

Rule 1-3 expresses the principle that golf is meant to be the same game for everyone, with the same code of Rules and the same set of penalties. It becomes a different game, for instance, when opponents agree that they'll concede each other every putt "within the leather." They've made an agreement to ignore Rule 1-1, and both should be disqualified.

Rule 1-3 is vital to the integrity of the game, so the interpretations have been consistently and properly strict. Key decisions:

- In a match player A, who won the last hole, says to B, "You hit first. I don't want the honor." B agrees and plays first.

Answer: They've agreed to waive Rule 10-1, which provides that the last player who won a hole is to play first on every hole until he loses one, and both are to be disqualified.

● A naughty thing happened in a regional competition. During a stroke-play round, a competitor failed to hole out once but continued to play the round. Her marker (another competitor in the same pairing) observed the violation but signed the score card anyway. Both were well aware of the violation.

Answer: Failing to hole out in stroke play is a violation calling for disqualification. In this case both are disqualified on the basis that they agreed to waive Rule 1-1.

1-4. Points Not Covered by Rules

No set of rules can cover every possible situation, and therefore it is sometimes necessary to rule "in equity." Here's a sampling:

● This actually happened. A woman took a hefty cut at a ball on an embankment. At first she couldn't find her ball, but then saw it stuck in the face of the club, held firmly by wet clay.

Answer: She should drop the ball as near as possible to the spot where the club was when the ball stuck to it. Here there is no penalty but, naturally, the stroke she made was counted.

● As a player putted, his caddie pulled the flagstick. The cup-liner came up with the flagstick, and the ball hit the cup-liner.

Answer: The cup should have been restored to its original position and the ball played from where it then lay—one foot from the hole—without penalty.

● As a player stepped into a bunker to play a shot, she noticed a rattlesnake near her ball. What to do?

Answer: It's not reasonable to expect a player to play from such a dangerous situation. The player is allowed to place a ball without penalty in the hazard, or in a similar nearby hazard, in a situation she does not regard as dangerous, as near as possible to the spot where the ball lay and in a lie similar to that which it originally occupied. The same applies to bees and wasps; indeed, a similar ruling was made for players in a bunker infested by yellow jackets in the 1949 Amateur Championship at the Oak Hill Country Club, Rochester, N.Y.

● A caddie for Lancy Smith, one of the best American women amateurs, accidentally kicked a coin marking the position of her opponent's ball closer to the hole.

Answer: The coin should be replaced as close as possible to the spot where it lay without penalty to anyone. A ball-marker is a movable obstruction and does not have the same status as a ball in play.

RULE 2

MATCH PLAY

2-1
Winner of Hole

In match play the game is played by holes.

Except as otherwise provided in the Rules, a hole is won by the side which holes its ball in the fewer strokes. In a handicap match the lower net score wins the hole.

A hole is halved if each side holes out in the same number of strokes.

When a player has holed out and his opponent has been left with a stroke for the half, if the player thereafter incurs a penalty, the hole is halved.

2-2
Halved Hole

The reckoning of holes is kept by the terms: so many "holes up" or "all square," and so many "to play."

A side is "dormie" when it is as many holes up as there are holes remaining to be played.

2-3
Reckoning of Holes

A match (which consists of a stipulated round, unless otherwise decreed by the Committee) is won by the side which is leading by a number of holes greater than the number of holes remaining to be played.

A side may concede a match at any time prior to the conclusion of the match.

The Committee may, for the purpose of settling a tie, extend the stipulated round to as many holes as are required for a match to be won.

2-4
Winner of Match

In match play, if a doubt or dispute arises between the players and no duly authorized representative of the Committee is available within a reasonable time, the players shall continue the match without delay. Any claim, if it is to be considered by the Committee, must be made before any player in the match plays from the next teeing ground or, in the case of the last hole of the match, before all players in the match leave the putting green.

No later claim shall be considered unless it is based on facts previously unknown to the player making the claim and the player making the claim had been given wrong information (Rules 6-2a and 9) by an opponent. In any case, no later claim shall be considered after the result of the match has been officially announced, unless the Committee is satisfied that the opponent knew he was giving wrong information.

2-5
Claims

The penalty for a breach of a Rule in match play is loss of hole except when otherwise provided.

2-6
General Penalty

One of golf's special appeals is that it can be played two ways. The outcome can be determined on the basis of holes won—match play —or by total number of strokes—stroke play. Arguments about the more valid form of play go on endlessly. I prefer stroke play, but I do not quarrel with the contention that match play (which is the only way golf was played for hundreds of years) is fascinating, calls for a different strategic approach and, above all, is intensely personal.

Rule 2-1 defines match play as the form of the game in which score is kept by the winning of holes rather than by total strokes. Rule 2-2 is a logical exception to the customary penalties in match play. There are occasions when, for example, player A has holed out in 4 and his opponent is left with a putt for a 4. Player A then violates a Rule—let's say he inadvertently moves the opponent's ball. That violation calls for a one-stroke penalty, which is not assessed in this instance. Since the best his opponent could possibly do is to make the putt and tie the hole, Rule 2-2 reasonably asserts that the hole is halved.

"Dormie" represents a curious case in which common and incorrect usage has virtually reversed the true meaning of a word. The player who is 6 holes up in match play with only 6 to play is the one who is dormie, not his opponent. The opponent might be said to be dormant.

What about the phrase "stipulated round" in Rule 2-4? Again, the Definitions are critical. The "stipulated round" requires that the holes be played in the correct sequence. A Decision tells how two players in a match somehow got lost after six holes and proceeded to play three holes other than the 7th, 8th and 9th. They then discovered the error and asked what to do.

Answer: Ignore the results of the three holes played out of sequence, go back and resume the match on the 7th hole and replay the holes played in error when they are reached.

Remember that the "stipulated round" starts on the 1st hole—not the 10th. Opponents in a club match who find that the 1st tee is backed up but the 10th is open need the approval of the Committee in order to begin a match on the back nine.

The first sentence of Rule 2-5 handles the everyday problem of what to do when opponents differ on a Rule or simply don't know the answer. They should continue play even though the status of the match is in doubt. The standing of the match is adjusted according to the ruling they receive later.

Focus on the word "claim" in Rule 2-5. It's synonymous with the more commonly used "call"—as in "I call this hole on you." Claims must be timely. If you see your opponent violate a Rule during the play of the second hole and that hole is halved or won by him, don't bother mentioning the violation during the play of the third hole. Too late. You can't hold your claim in reserve, and all you've done is create a chilled atmosphere.

On the other hand, if your opponent violated a Rule during the second hole and you weren't aware at the time but learned of the violation later, the clock hasn't run out on your right to claim. We'll get to that in Rule 34.

Violations generally call for loss of hole in match play. Exceptions to the general penalty are specified in certain Rules. An example occurs in Rule 18 when a player accidentally moves his ball. It's a one-stroke penalty, not loss of hole, and the ball must be replaced.

RULE 3

STROKE PLAY

3-1
Winner

The competitor who plays the <u>stipulated round</u> or rounds in the fewest strokes is the winner.

If a competitor fails to hole out at any hole before he has played a <u>stroke</u> from the next <u>teeing ground</u> or, in the case of the last hole of the round, before he has left the <u>putting green</u>, *he shall be disqualified.*

3-2

Failure to Hole Out

In stroke play only, when during play of a hole a competitor is doubtful of his rights or procedure, he may, without penalty, play a second ball. After the doubtful situation has arisen and before taking further action, he should announce to his marker his decision to proceed under this Rule and which ball he will score with if the Rules permit.

On completing the round, the competitor shall report the facts immediately to the <u>Committee</u>; if he fails to do so, *he shall be disqualified.* If the Rules allow the procedure selected in advance by the competitor, the score with the ball selected shall be his score for the hole. If the competitor fails to announce in advance his procedure or selection, the ball with the higher score shall count if the Rules allow the procedure adopted for such ball.

Note: *A second ball played under Rule 3-3 is not a provisional ball under Rule 27-2.*

3-3

Doubt as to Procedure

If a competitor refuses to comply with a Rule affecting the rights of another competitor, *he shall be disqualified.*

3-4

Refusal to Comply with a Rule

The penalty for a breach of a Rule in stroke play is two strokes except when otherwise provided.

3-5

General Penalty

Stroke play is commonly called "medal play"—a term derived from the old British custom of playing occasional one-day competitions for the prize of a medal. (My permanent prize for winning the 1982 U.S. Open, by the way, is the USGA's gold medal.) Until the eighteenth century, when golf was already hundreds of years old, the game was always played at match play. Stroke play was inspired by the need for a means of completing a tournament in only one day.

Match play was still the preferred style of play when the USGA established its championships in 1895. The first U.S. Amateur was played at match play, and the next day the U.S. Open was tagged on almost as an afterthought at stroke play (thirty-six holes in one day so the ten competing pros wouldn't be away too long from their shops).

A classic application of Rule 3-2 occurred on the final hole of the playoff for the 1962 U.S. Open at Oakmont, near Pittsburgh. Jack Nicklaus, a twenty-one-year-old rookie pro, needed to hole a putt of only three feet for a 71. Jack had marked the position of his ball with a coin. Meanwhile, Arnold Palmer was lining up a longer putt, which he made for a 74. He then graciously picked up Jack's coin as an act of concession. Joseph C. Dey, Jr., former USGA executive director, immediately ordered Jack to replace the coin and hole out. You see, there is no such animal in stroke play as a concession. Technically, if

29

Jack had walked off the 18th green without holing out, he could have been disqualified.

3-3. Doubt as to Procedure

The privilege of playing a second ball applies only in stroke play and not in match play. Why not in match play? Because the essence of match play is that players should know the status of the match. The introduction of a second ball erodes that right. The vital element of strategy in match play goes out the window if a player has to play against two balls, not knowing which one counts.

An application of Rule 3-3 might go like this: Your ball is embedded on a closely mown slope near a stream, but you don't know if the ball is within the hazard or not because the Committee has been remiss in its duty to define the margin of the hazard.

If the ball is within the hazard, you're out of luck. If it's outside the hazard, you're entitled to relief without penalty (see Rule 25-2). So tell your marker you are going to invoke this Rule, and don't forget to state the obvious—that you want the score with the *second* ball to count.

Then play both balls into the hole—the first under the premise that it was within the hazard and the second as if you were entitled to a free drop.

When you've finished the round, dump the case into the lap of the Committee. It's up to them to decide whether your original ball was within the hazard.

By the way, if you happen to hole out your next stroke with the original ball but take 5 to get down with the second ball, you will be in the curious position of hoping the Committee finds no merit in your earlier argument that the ball was not in the hazard.

3-4. Refusal to Comply with a Rule

Frankly, I've never seen an occasion when this Rule had to be applied. It could happen, I suppose, if a hardheaded player who thinks he knows the Rules refuses to lift his ball on the apron of a putting green when asked to do so by another player who is about to play on that line, a right granted in Rule 22. Hardhead is disqualified.

3-5. General Penalty

Violations in stroke play generally call for two strokes, but some transgressions call for disqualification. One example of the latter is practicing on the course itself on the day of a competition. An example of a one-stroke penalty occurs when a player, his partner or the caddie accidentally moves the players' ball.

CLUBS AND THE BALL

The United States Golf Association and the Royal and Ancient Golf Club of St. Andrews reserve the right to change the Rules and make and change the interpretations relating to clubs, balls and other implements at any time.

RULE 4

CLUBS

If a manufacturer is in doubt as to whether a club which he proposes to manufacture conforms with Rule 4 and Appendix II,* he should submit a sample to the United States Golf Association for a ruling, such sample to become its property for reference purposes.

A player in doubt as to the conformity of a club should consult the United States Golf Association.

A club is an implement designed to be used for striking the ball.

A putter is a club designed primarily for use on the putting green.

The player's clubs shall conform with the provisions of this Rule and with the specifications and interpretations set forth in Appendix II.

a. GENERAL

The club shall be composed of a shaft and a head. All parts

4-1

Form and Make of Clubs

---

* Hereafter when in the text of the Rules themselves reference is made to Appendices, please note that these may be found in the USGA's *Rules of Golf* booklet.

Illegal Clubs

Most of these clubs, for a variety of reasons, do not conform to the Rules of Golf. They're on display at the USGA Museum—open daily to the public without charge—at Far Hills, New Jersey. Incidentally, that piece of plumbing second from the bottom is actually a putter (one of many) sent to Arnold Palmer with the thought that it might cure his problems on the greens. Arnold lent many of the more imaginative gifts to the USGA. (R. 4)

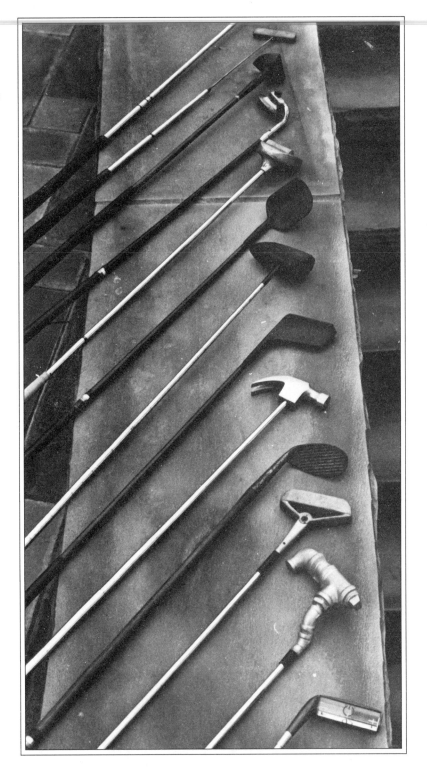

of the club shall be fixed so that the club is one unit. The club shall not be designed to be adjustable except for weight. The club shall not be substantially different from the traditional and customary form and make.

b. SHAFT

The shaft shall be generally straight, with the same bending and twisting properties in any direction, and shall be attached to the clubhead at the heel either directly or through a single plain neck or socket. A putter shaft may be attached to any point in the head.

c. GRIP

The grip consists of that part of the shaft designed to be held by the player and any material added to it for the purpose of obtaining a firm hold. The grip shall be substantially straight and plain in form and shall not be molded for any part of the hands.

d. CLUBHEAD

The length of the clubhead, from heel to toe, shall be greater than the breadth from face to back. The clubhead shall be generally plain in shape.

The clubhead shall have only one face designed for striking the ball, except that a putter may have two such faces if the loft of each is substantially the same and does not exceed ten degrees.

e. CLUB FACE

The face shall not have any degree of concavity and, in relation to the ball, shall be hard and rigid. It shall be generally smooth except for such markings as are permitted by Appendix II. If the basic structural material of the head and face of a club, other than a putter, is metal, no inset or attachment is permitted.

f. WEAR

A club which conforms to Rule 4-1 when new is deemed to conform after wear through normal use. Any part of a club which has been purposely altered is regarded as new and must conform, in the altered state, to the Rules.

g. DAMAGE

A club which ceases to conform to Rule 4-1 because of damage sustained in the normal course of play may be used in its damaged state, but only for the remainder of the stipulated round during which such damage was sustained. A club which ceases to conform because of damage sustained other than in the normal course of play shall not be used unless it is repaired so as to conform to Rule 4-1.

4-2
Playing Characteristics Not to Be Changed

During a stipulated round, the playing characteristics of a club shall not be purposely changed, except that damage occurring during such round may be repaired, provided play is not unduly delayed. Damage which occurred prior to the round may be repaired, provided the playing characteristics are not changed.

4-3

Foreign Material

No foreign material shall be applied to the club face for the purpose of influencing the movement of the ball.

PENALTY FOR BREACH OF RULE 4-1, -2 OR -3:
Disqualification.

4-4

Maximum of Fourteen Clubs

a. SELECTION AND REPLACEMENT OF CLUBS

The player shall start a <u>stipulated round</u> with not more than fourteen clubs. He is limited to the clubs thus selected for that round except that, without unduly delaying play, he may:

(i) if he started with fewer than fourteen, add as many as will bring his total to that number; and

(ii) replace, with any club, a club which becomes unfit for play in the normal course of play.

The addition or replacement of a club or clubs may not be made by borrowing from any other person playing on the course.

b. PARTNERS MAY SHARE CLUBS

Partners may share clubs, provided that the total number of clubs carried by the partners so sharing does not exceed fourteen.

PENALTY FOR BREACH OF RULE 4-4a OR b, REGARDLESS OF NUMBER OF EXCESS CLUBS CARRIED:

Match play—At the conclusion of the hole at which the breach is discovered, the state of the match shall be adjusted by deducting one hole for each hole at which a breach occurred. Maximum deduction per round: two holes.
Stroke play—Two strokes for each hole at which any breach occurred; maximum penalty per round: four strokes.
Bogey and par competitions—Penalties as in match play.
Stableford competitions—See Rule 32-1b.

c. EXCESS CLUB DECLARED OUT OF PLAY

Any club carried or used in breach of this Rule shall be declared out of play by the player immediately upon discovery that a breach has occurred and thereafter shall not be used by the player during the round *under penalty of disqualification.*

Rules 4 and 5 exist in order to preserve the challenge of the game. Without reasonable standards, space-age technology might lead to new kinds of clubs and balls that would change the very nature of the game. An armaments race in golf makes no sense at all.

The USGA's annual budget for equipment testing and research is more than half a million dollars, money well-spent.

4-1. Form and Make of Clubs

Sophisticated golfers who used to worry about the grooves in their iron clubs becoming too wide through wear no longer need to worry. Rule 4-1f affirms that the club remains legal so long as it was okay when new and it became worn from normal use.

4-2. Playing Characteristics Not to Be Changed

An example of a violation of this Rule would be the addition of lead tape to a driver *during* a round. It's all right to add or remove tape *before* a round.

4-3. Foreign Material

The prohibitions against applying "foreign material" to the club face or the ball are reactions against imaginative golfers who applied materials such as chalk or Vaseline in order, they claimed, to get more distance or to keep the ball on a straighter line by reducing spin. When I played on the Stanford University golf team, teammate Sandy Adelman spit on the face of his driver on every tee. That was before the USGA issued a Rules of Golf Decision on that very point. Sandy Adelman might not agree, but the USGA insists that "saliva is considered foreign material."

4-4. Maximum of Fourteen Clubs

There was no limit on the number of clubs until 1938. The ceiling was established because some players had gone to extremes in terms of carrying "specialty" clubs, supposedly designed to fit every kind of shot. Golf bags were becoming arsenals. Lawson Little and Craig Wood, two of the stars of the 1930s, went forth to battle with twenty-five clubs each. On the other hand, when Francis Ouimet won the 1913 U.S. Open, his ten-year-old caddie Eddie Lowery carried only seven clubs.

The number fourteen was selected as the maximum because it corresponded to what was generally thought to be a standard set of clubs. Most touring pros carry irons numbered 1 through 9, pitching and sand wedges, a putter and only two woods.

Applying penalties for violations of Rule 4-4 can be tricky. Suppose in a match, player A is 2-up against B after sixteen holes. They discover on the 17th tee that A has been carrying fifteen clubs. The status of the match immediately becomes even, since A gets the maximum penalty—loss of two holes.

Another example: A wins the first hole of a match against B, who then finds he's got an extra club. Poor B goes from 1 down to 2 down even though he's only played one hole, since the penalty is applied to the state of the match at the conclusion of the hole. Incidentally, they don't skip the second hole; the match resumes on the second tee with the penalty added.

There have been inadvertent and odd violations of Rule 4-4 on the tour. I was paired with Johnny Miller in the first round of the 1976 World Series of Golf when he suffered the maximum penalty of four strokes. As we were playing the 18th hole, Johnny noticed a tiny club in the bottom of his bag. It was an old Bull's-Eye putter he had modified for his son. In fact it was nothing but grip and head, about eighteen inches long. Nevertheless, it was a golf club and it changed Johnny's 72 into a 76. Unfair? Not necessarily. As a matter of fact, I often play with a friend who crouches over a putter that's not much longer than the one Johnny cut down for his son.

Just about every player I know has carried an extra club or more at some time. It happened to me once—in a qualifying round for the Missouri Amateur Championship. I managed to go out with eighteen clubs. At that time the penalty called for a maximum of four penalty

Iron Byron

There's no other machine quite like the USGA's Iron Byron, the USGA's mechanical golfer, which plays on a course all its own—a test range at USGA headquarters. The prototype was built to emulate the swing of my friend and mentor Byron Nelson. The USGA machine is rigged with a laser beam and high-speed photo equipment. Every hit is dissected to the extent of a recording of the speed of the club at impact (in millionths of a second) and wind velocity (both horizontally and vertically) during the six seconds the ball is in flight. During the USGA Overall Distance Standard tests, a ball is teed just after being removed from an incubator where it was stored at 75°F. When the clubhead strikes the ball, it will be moving at 109 miles per hour—about the clubhead speed of a long driver on the Tour.

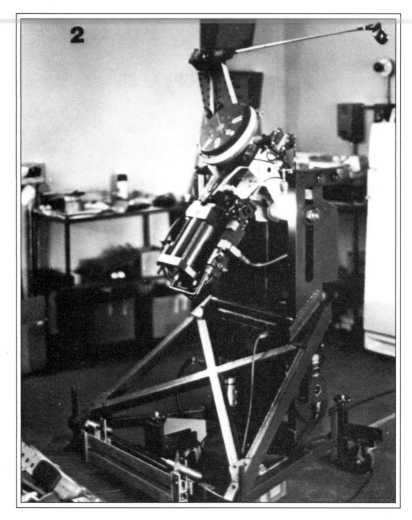

strokes for every extra club. My 76 was converted into a nifty 92. That's the last time I or my caddie forgot to count my clubs before starting a round.

The penalty for an extra club was applied once even to Jack Nicklaus, who is a paragon when it comes to being meticulous. It happened this way: Jack and David Graham, who use the same brand of irons, were examining and discussing each other's clubs at a practice putting green. David's pitching wedge somehow found its way into Jack's bag, and Jack made the discovery on the first hole.

Rule 4-4 limits you to the fourteen clubs you start with unless a club "becomes unfit for play in the normal course of play." When a shaft breaks as you're playing a stroke, you are entitled to a substitute, but you can't delay play or borrow a club from another on the course. On the other hand, snapping a putter over your knee is not considered "in the normal course of play."

Millions of TV viewers saw Ray Floyd accidentally break the shaft of an iron club against a tree in the last round of the 1983 Tournament of Champions at La Costa. The incident happened on the last hole, so Raymond was not concerned about a replacement. But had it occurred, say, on the 9th hole, Raymond could have sent back into the pro shop or locker room for another club, and it could have been any club he desired—a wood or even a second putter—to bring his total up to fourteen.

RULE 5

THE BALL

The ball the player uses shall conform to specifications set forth in Appendix III on maximum weight, minimum size, spherical symmetry, initial velocity and overall distance when tested under specified conditions.

5-1
General

No foreign material shall be applied to a ball for the purpose of changing its playing characteristics.
PENALTY FOR BREACH OF RULE 5-1 OR 5-2:
Disqualification.

5-2
Foreign Material Prohibited

A ball is unfit for play if it is visibly cut or out of shape or so cracked, pierced or otherwise damaged as to interfere with its true flight or true roll or its normal behavior when struck. A ball is not unfit for play solely because mud or other materials adhere to it, its surface is scratched or its paint is damaged or discolored.

If a player has reason to believe his ball has become unfit for play during play of the hole being played, he may during the play of such hole lift his ball without penalty to determine whether it is unfit, provided he announces his intention in advance to his opponent in match play or his marker or a fellow-competitor in stroke play and gives his opponent, marker or fellow-competitor an opportunity to examine the ball. If he lifts the ball without announcing his intention in advance or giving his opponent, marker or fellow-competitor an opportunity to examine the ball, *he shall incur a penalty of one stroke.*

If it is determined that the ball has become unfit for play during play of the hole being played, the player may substitute another ball, placing it on the spot where the original ball lay. Otherwise, the original ball shall be replaced.

If a ball breaks into pieces as a result of a stroke, the stroke shall be replayed without penalty (see Rule 20-5).
* PENALTY FOR BREACH OF RULE 5-3:
Match play—Loss of hole; Stroke play—Two strokes.

5-3
Ball Unfit for Play

* If a player incurs the general penalty for breach of Rule 5-3, no additional penalty under the Rule shall be applied.

Note 1: The ball may not be cleaned to determine whether it is unfit for play—see Rule 21.

Note 2: If the opponent, marker or fellow-competitor wishes to dispute a claim of unfitness, he must do so before the player plays another ball.

On a worldwide basis the size of the ball is the only difference in the Rules of Golf. In Great Britain and other countries adhering to the Rules of the Royal and Ancient Golf Club of St. Andrews, the ball may be as small as 1.62 inches in diameter, compared to our minimum diameter of 1.68 inches.

While the small ball is still used in Great Britain and other countries, the bigger ball is now standard in professional tours throughout the world, including Great Britain and Europe.

The 6/100 of an inch can make quite a difference. I once used the small ball while winning a tournament in Japan. I could have used either ball in that event but settled on the small one because it makes the game easier. The 1.62-inch ball goes farther (about 5 percent for me), it minimizes hooks and slices, and it bores into the wind better, but it is harder to maneuver.

The small ball shows up occasionally in this country. The penalty for using it is properly severe—disqualification—since the user has an advantage equivalent to teeing up many yards ahead of the tee-marker.

Not long ago a spate of mail-order magazine ads appeared for un-named brands of balls, promising extra distance, and alerting, or teasing, the reader to the truth that the ball is not approved by the USGA. The kicker "for tournament play" was sometimes appended. Some of these balls are nothing more than 1.62-inch balls. It's true they don't conform to USGA Rules, but almost all golfers rely on the Rules of Golf in everyday play and not just in competitions. A score made with a 1.62-inch ball can't be turned in for USGA handicap purposes either.

5-3. Ball Unfit for Play

Rule 5-3 begins with a commonsense definition of "unfit for play." An opponent, marker or fellow-competitor has the right to question a judgment that a ball is unfit for play.

This Rule was strengthened in 1984. It now holds that a player who thinks his ball may be unfit for play and wants to examine it must not only announce his intention before lifting the ball but also give his opponent, marker or fellow-competitor an opportunity to examine the condition of the lifted ball. If he fails to do so, there is a one-stroke penalty—even if the ball does prove, in fact, to be unfit for play.

The advent of balls with plastic cores and of one-piece balls prompted the Rulesmakers to establish that when a ball breaks into pieces, the stroke is canceled.

I'm finicky about the balls I use on the tour. Most of us put a brand-new ball into play on every fourth hole. Moreover, I won't use a ball on a subsequent hole after I've scarred it playing a bunker shot. I probably average eight balls a round.

PLAYER'S RESPONSIBILITIES

RULE 6

THE PLAYER

A "marker" is one who is appointed by the Committee to record a competitor's score in stroke play. He may be a fellow-competitor. He is not a referee.

A marker should not lift a ball or mark its position unless authorized to do so by the competitor and, unless he is a fellow-competitor, should not attend the flagstick or stand at the hole or mark its position.

Definition

The player is responsible for knowing the conditions under which the competition is to be played (Rule 33-1).

6-1
Conditions of Competition

a. MATCH PLAY

Before starting a match in a handicap competition, the player shall declare to his opponent the handicap to which he is entitled under the conditions of the competition. If a player declares and begins the match with a higher handicap which would affect the number of strokes given or received, *he shall be disqualified;* otherwise, the player shall play off the declared handicap.

b. STROKE PLAY

In any round of a handicap competition, the competitor shall ensure that the handicap to which he is entitled under the conditions of the competition is recorded on his score card before it is returned to the Committee. If no handicap is recorded on his score card before it is returned, or if the

6-2
Handicap

39

recorded handicap is higher than that to which he is entitled and this affects the number of strokes received, *he shall be disqualified* from that round of the handicap competition; otherwise, the score shall stand.

Note: *It is the player's responsibility to know the holes at which handicap strokes are to be given or received.*

6-3 Time of Starting and Groups

a. TIME OF STARTING

The player shall start at the time laid down by the Committee.

b. GROUPS

In stroke play, the competitor shall remain throughout the round in the group arranged by the Committee unless the Committee authorizes or ratifies a change.

PENALTY FOR BREACH OF RULE 6-3: *Disqualification.*

(Best-ball and four-ball play—see Rules 30-3a and 31-2.)

Note: *The Committee may provide in the conditions of a competition (Rule 33-1) that, in the absence of circumstances which warrant waiving the penalty of disqualification as provided in Rule 33-7, if the player arrives at his starting point, ready to play, within five minutes of his starting time, the penalty for failure to start on time is* loss of the first hole to be played in match play or two strokes in stroke play *instead of disqualification.*

6-4 Caddie

The player may have only one caddie at any one time, *under penalty of disqualification.*

For any breach of a Rule by his caddie, the player incurs the relative penalty.

6-5 Ball

The responsibility for playing the proper ball rests with the player. Each player should put an identification mark on his ball.

6-6 Scoring in Stroke Play

a. RECORDING SCORES

After each hole the marker should check the score with the competitor. On completion of the round the marker shall sign the card and hand it to the competitor; if more than one marker records the scores, each shall sign for the part for which he is responsible.

b. CHECKING SCORES

The competitor shall check his score for each hole, settle any doubtful points with the Committee, ensure that the marker has signed the card, countersign the card himself and return it to the Committee as soon as possible. The competitor is responsible for the correctness of the score recorded for each hole.

PENALTY FOR BREACH OF RULE 6-6b: *Disqualification.*

Note: *As to the Committee's responsibility to add the scores and apply the recorded handicap, see Rule 33-5.*

c. NO ALTERATION OF SCORES

No alteration may be made on a card after the competitor has returned it to the Committee.

If the competitor returns a score for any hole lower than actually taken, *he shall be disqualified.* If he returns a score for any hole higher than actually taken, the score as returned shall stand.

Note: *In four-ball stroke play, see also Rule 31-4 and -7a.*

The player shall play without undue delay. Between completion of a hole and playing from the next teeing ground, the player shall not unduly delay play.

6-7
Undue Delay

PENALTY FOR BREACH OF RULE 6-7:
Match play—Loss of hole; Stroke play—Two strokes. For repeated offense—Disqualification.
If the player unduly delays play between holes, he is delaying the play of the next hole and the penalty applies to that hole.

a. WHEN PERMITTED

6-8
Discontinuance of Play

The player shall not discontinue play unless:
 (i) the Committee has suspended play;
 (ii) he believes there is danger from lightning;
 (iii) he is seeking a decision from the Committee on a doubtful or disputed point (see Rules 2-5 and 34-3); or
 (iv) there is some other good reason such as sudden illness.
Bad weather is not of itself a good reason for discontinuing play.

If the player discontinues play without specific permission from the Committee, he shall report to the Committee as soon as practicable. If he does so and the Committee considers his reason satisfactory, the player incurs no penalty. Otherwise, *the player shall be disqualified.*

Exception in match play: Players discontinuing match play by agreement are not subject to disqualification unless by so doing the competition is delayed.

Note: *Leaving the course does not of itself constitute discontinuance of play.*

b. PROCEDURE

When play is discontinued in accordance with the Rules, it should, if feasible, be discontinued after the completion of the play of a hole. If this is not feasible, the player should lift his ball. The ball may be cleaned when so lifted. If a ball has been so lifted, the player shall, when play is resumed, place a ball on the spot from which the original ball was lifted.

PENALTY FOR BREACH OF RULE 6-8b:
Match play—Loss of hole; Stroke play—Two strokes.

Rule 6 contains a potpourri of items that have nothing to do with striking the ball, or with where it goes, but which nonetheless are essential to orderly and sound procedure. The provisions of Rule 6 underscore the principle that golf is a game that can be carried on only if the players act responsibly. This is not a game in which secretaries cater to the whims of stars. You have to get there on your own.

6-1. Conditions of Competition

Golf administrators use the phrase "conditions of play." These include the essentials: form of play (match or stroke, individual or team); whether or not it's a handicap event, and if so, what form; who is eligible; the dates and the starting times; whether there's an entry fee; and the prizes. It's up to the player to learn the conditions.

6-2. Handicap

The imperative word *shall* is used to require match play opponents to inform each other of their handicaps before play begins. Incidentally, the USGA Handicap System—which is nationally accepted—recommends that current handicaps be used for each round. In a handicap competition played over a period of weeks, the handicaps can go up or down with each revision.

In stroke play competitions, there is a strict provision that the handicaps in effect for each round be noted on the score cards returned to the Committee.

6-3. Time of Starting and Groups

One of the most publicized instances of a player missing his starting time came in the 1980 U.S. Open at Baltusrol, when Seve Ballesteros rushed to the first tee—too late.

A Committee will waive the disqualification penalty for good reason. Example? You're trapped for hours in a motel elevator. But running out of gas, getting lost or your alarm failing to work are examples of personal snafus that will not cut it with Committees.

6-4. Caddie

A player and his caddie are an integral and intimate unit, and they share responsibility for upholding the Rules. For example, if a caddie steps on a scruff mark on the player's line of putt, the player is penalized.

My regular tour caddie is Bruce Edwards. I trust him implicitly. Bruce has never cost me a penalty stroke.

Touring pro Jodie Mudd was less fortunate at the 1983 Heritage Classic. Jodie was near the lead in the midst of his second round when we had an interruption of play because of bad weather. When the signal was given to resume play, Jodie returned to the course promptly, but his caddie, who had Jodie's clubs, was late in getting there. Jodie was disqualified.

6-5. Ball

The Rules, in this instance, use the word "should" rather than "shall," so it's not a violation if you don't put a distinctive mark on your ball. But suppose you're playing Brand X, with a number 1 on it, and you yank your drive into the rough. When you get to the likely spot, you find two Brand X number 1s. What you've got on your hands is a lost ball—unless you can with certainty identify your ball. My identifying marks are a couple of pencil-point marks in the dimple on the right of the number on each ball.

6-6. Scoring in Stroke Play

These provisions are limited to stroke play because scoring in match play depends entirely on the opponents' agreement or understanding as to the status of the match. It's wise to keep a score card during a match, but the card itself has no official status and it need not be signed or turned in. You need only present the result to the Committee.

As for stroke play, the application of Rule 6-6 has prompted some of the most celebrated Rules controversies in the history of the game. Roberto deVicenzo should have tied Bob Goalby for first in the 1968 Masters and played off the next day, but Roberto, who had made a birdie 3 on the 17th hole, countersigned the card prepared by Tommy Aaron, his marker, which erroneously showed 4 in the box for the 17th hole. According to Rule 6-6, the higher score had to stand, and the one-stroke difference made Roberto the runner-up.

Back in 1957, a similarly unhappy incident involved Jackie Pung. She was disqualified from the Women's Open Championship because she countersigned a card that had her making a 5 at the 4th hole, where she had actually made a 6. The total on the card was correct. A simple error of transposition had been made by her marker. Mrs. Pung's card should have read "5–6" for two successive holes, but instead it read "6–5."

Personally, I'll take Rule 6-6 just the way it is. It gives me the absolute right to be responsible for my score. I don't have to sign the card until and unless I'm satisfied with what it shows. Any alteration would erode that privilege.

The marker in tour events is always another player in the same group. A scorer accompanies each group. The card the scorer maintains is the source of scores for the scoreboards and the media. As soon as I finish, I always double-check my score card by first circling and checking my birdies and bogeys and then going over the card hole by hole with the unofficial scorer.

Actually, the most common cause for disqualification under Rule 6-6 is forgetting to sign the card. That's the first and last thing I think about in the scoring tent. So far I've never been disqualified for turning in an incorrect card or failing to sign one.

6-7. Undue Delay

In my view, golf has been allowed to become too slow a game, and I tend to think golf associations, including both the USGA and the PGA Tour, have been too cautious about imposing penalties for slow play.

6-8. Discontinuance of Play

Discontinuing play, the subject of Rule 6-8, is often a touchy question in club match play when one player or team wants to stop and the other wants to continue. Let's assume it's raining hard but that the course remains eminently playable. If a Committee has not suspended play in a storm *without* lightning, the side that wants to forge on has the right to do so. But note the General Exception to the effect that in match play opponents can by mutual agreement suspend play, provided that they don't cause the competition to be delayed.

Lightning is, of course, bad news. Rule 6-8 gives any player the right to stop when "he believes there is danger from lightning." He doesn't have to consult with his opponents, fellow-competitors or the Committee.

During the 1975 Western Open, Lee Trevino, Jerry Heard and Bobby Nichols were all hurt when a bolt of lightning struck near their improvised shelter from the storm while play was suspended. Every year golfers are killed by lightning, and it's impossible to be overly cautious. When I saw a flash during the fourth round of the 1983 Open at Oakmont, I stopped immediately, even though my ball was on the 15th green, thirty feet from the hole. I marked my ball and took off. The USGA siren sounded a few seconds later. The next morning, when play resumed, I had the unique and unwanted experience of beginning play with a long, slick putt.

The USGA issues a poster on protection from lightning storms that should be prominently displayed in every locker room.

RULE 7

PRACTICE

7-1

Before or Between Rounds

a. MATCH PLAY

On any day of a match play competition, a player may practice on the competition <u>course</u> before a round.

b. STROKE PLAY

On any day of a stroke competition or playoff, a competitor shall not practice on the competition <u>course</u> or test the surface of any putting green on the course before a round or playoff. When two or more rounds of a stroke competition are to be played over consecutive days, practice between those rounds on any competition course remaining to be played is prohibited.

Exception: Practice putting or chipping on or near the first <u>teeing ground</u> before starting a round or playoff is permitted.

PENALTY FOR BREACH OF RULE 7-1b: *Disqualification.*

Note: *The Committee may in the conditions of a competition (Rule 33-1) prohibit practice on the competition course on any day of a match play competition or permit practice on the competition course or part of the course (Rule 33-2c) on any day of or between rounds of a stroke competition.*

7-2

During Round

A player shall not play a practice <u>stroke</u> either during the play of a hole or between the play of two holes except that, between the play of two holes, the player may practice putting or chipping on or near the <u>putting green</u> of the hole last played, any practice putting green or the <u>teeing ground</u> of the next hole to be played in the round, provided such practice stroke is not played from a hazard and does not unduly delay play (Rule 6-7).

Exception: When play has been suspended by the Committee, a player may, prior to resumption of play, practice (a) as provided in this Rule, (b) anywhere other than on the competition course and (c) as otherwise permitted by the Committee.

PENALTY FOR BREACH OF RULE 7-2:
Match play—Loss of hole; Stroke play—Two strokes.
In the event of a breach between the play of two holes, the penalty applies to the next hole.
Note 1: *A practice swing is not a practice* stroke *and may be taken at any place, provided the player does not breach the Rules.*
Note 2: *The Committee may prohibit practice on or near the* putting green *of the hole last played.*

The language of Rule 7 is finicky—and well it might be, since golf is an exercise in finite judgments and muscle memory skills. If you could rehearse each shot before playing it, golf would be a different and easier game. I've averaged a fraction more than 70 strokes a round on the tour in recent years. If the Rules allowed me to practice each shot one time before it counted, I think I could reduce that average to 66.

7-1. Before or Between Rounds

This aspect of the rules was revised in 1984 to point up the contrast between the match play and stroke play restrictions on practice.

In match play, you are not prohibited from practicing on the course prior to a round. But in stroke play you are. Why? Opponents in a match obviously start at the same time and therefore have the same opportunity to go out and try some or all of the course in advance. But in stroke play, those with early starting times would not have the same opportunity to practice on-course as those with later times.

The Rule, however, gives the Committee the option of flopping both conditions. That is, practice on the course in match play may be banned and, conversely, may be allowed in stroke play. When that happens, it's up to the Committee to notify the players in the form of a condition of the competition.

Watch out for Rule 7-1 when you're involved in a 36-hole stroke play qualifying event over a weekend. You may play the first round Saturday morning and decide to go on the course Saturday afternoon for some practice. Don't! The penalty is disqualification unless the Committee specifically has said otherwise.

7-2. During Round

The wording of Rule 7-2 allows for such innocuous acts as chipping near or on a tee when you're delayed. It also permits you to practice-putt (or -chip) on the hole you've just completed—assuming you don't play from a hazard and can do so without delaying play. On the pro tour, putting practice is prohibited, as Note 2 contemplates, because it might delay play. Besides, all that extra traffic in the critical area near the hole would roughen the surface to the detriment of those who have late starting times.

The application of the penalty for a violation of Rule 7-2 is curious. Suppose a player replays a bunker shot on the 4th hole, which he's just won in a match. That's a clear-cut violation, since he's played a practice stroke in a hazard, but which hole does he lose? The penalty applies to the *next* hole, which means that he and his opponent skip hole 5 entirely and proceed directly to the 6th tee.

The Rules of Golf Committee is often forced to weave its way through thickets of technicalities in interpreting the Rules. Here are a couple of examples under the practice category:

● A man habitually tossed down plastic balls and hit them in the direction of the hole. His opponents complained bitterly. The player said swatting at plastic balls was not covered in the Rules of Golf. The USGA ruled that the player was in fact playing practice strokes in violation of Rule 7-2.

● A letter described a driving range adjacent to a fairway, and how a woman, after playing her second shot to the green, flicked a ball with a red band painted on it back to where it belonged on a practice range. This happened during stroke play, and the Committee socked her with two strokes. She took her case to the USGA, which ordained that "casually flicking a range ball, apparently only for the purpose of tidying up the course, should not be considered a violation." The Decision carefully pointed out that "under some circumstances" hitting a range ball back to the range would be a violation. Suppose the next shot calls for a carry of 190 yards over water, and the player carefully addresses a range ball with a 3-wood and bashes it back toward the practice tee.

● Then there is the notorious case of two prominent professionals, who shall not be named, who got out of sorts with each other. Player A, celebrated for his desire to play fast, was impatient with the group ahead and drove his ball before all three ahead played their second shots. Whereupon Player B addressed A's ball in the fairway and slammed it back at A, some 230 yards away, on the tee. The USGA ruled that B's act did not constitute practice but that it most certainly constituted a breach in accepted decorum and that in equity the Committee should impose the general penalty of two strokes.

RULE 8

ADVICE; INDICATING LINE OF PLAY

Definition

"Advice" is any counsel or suggestion which could influence a player in determining his play, the choice of a club or the method of making a <u>stroke</u>.

Information on the Rules or on matters of public information, such as the position of hazards or the flagstick on the putting green, is not advice.

8-1

Advice

Except as provided in Rule 8-2, a player may give advice to, or ask for advice from, only his partner or either of their caddies.

Note: *In a team competition without concurrent individual competition, the Committee may in the conditions of the competition (Rule 33-1) permit each team to appoint one per-*

son, e.g., *team captain or coach, who may give advice to members of that team. Such person shall be identified to the Committee prior to the start of the competition.*

a. OTHER THAN ON PUTTING GREEN

Except on the putting green, a player may have the line of play indicated to him by anyone, but no one shall stand on or close to the line while the stroke is being played. Any mark placed during the play of a hole by the player or with his knowledge to indicate the line shall be removed before the stroke is played.

Exception: Flagstick attended or held up—Rule 17-1.

b. ON THE PUTTING GREEN

When the player's ball is on the putting green, the player's caddie, his partner or his partner's caddie may, before the stroke is played, point out a line for putting, but in so doing the putting green shall not be touched in front of, to the side of, or behind the hole. No mark shall be placed anywhere on the putting green to indicate a line for putting.

PENALTY FOR BREACH OF RULE:

Match play—Loss of hole; Stroke play—Two strokes.

8-2
Indicating Line of Play

8-1. Advice

I seem to be allergic to the advice Rule. During the 1968 Amateur Championship at the Scioto Country Club in Columbus, Ohio, I was paired with Mike Taylor, another young amateur, from Mississippi. We hit it off well. On one hole I yelled clear across a fairway to ask Mike what he'd hit, and he answered. USGA official Pete Tufts could hardly believe his ears. Mike and I were each penalized two strokes—I for asking for advice, and Mike for giving it.

Then, twelve years later, I was cruising with a big lead in the last round of the 1980 Tournament of Champions. I was paired with Lee Trevino, who was struggling that day. I noticed a little swing flaw Lee seemed to have picked up and told him about it.

Bob Goalby, working as a roving announcer for NBC, heard of our exchange and commented on it as an illustration of the kind of good feeling that exists on the tour—not as a violation of the Rules.

Some landmark interpretations of Rule 8:

• A player in a college match had a delicate 40-yard pitch shot to execute. He approved and watched with great interest as a teammate, at that point a spectator following the match, dropped a ball and played the shot. His opponents protested vehemently. The player, who may well have benefited from his teammate's action, should have been disqualified from the hole if he did not try to stop such an irregular procedure.

• A player wanted to take a lesson between rounds of a 36-hole match for his club championship. That's okay, because the ban against receiving advice applies only during the stipulated round, which consists of 18 holes. As a matter of fact, Jerry Pate skipped lunch between rounds of the final match of the 1974 U.S. Amateur, which he won, in order to take a lesson from Conrad Rehling, his college coach.

● A double caddie often finds himself in a delicate position. Player A asks their caddie what club player B, his opponent, just hit. It's no violation, because the definition of "caddie" told us that a double caddie "is always deemed to be the caddie of the player whose ball is involved." Since it was his ball that was involved, player A was entitled to attempt to pry loose any useful information the caddie possessed.

Plenty of TV viewers, however, pounced on Goalby's remark and called both NBC and the club. When I finished the round, but before I signed my score card, tour official Jack Tuthill told me about the calls and asked if I'd given Trevino advice. I said I had. Jack said, "Add 2 strokes." Thank goodness I had a 3-stroke lead. Since he had not asked for advice, Trevino wasn't penalized.

A golfer may, of course, ask his caddie for advice. He can also seek help from his partner or his partner's caddie. A partner, remember, is someone on your side. Neither Mike Taylor nor Lee Trevino was my partner; we were fellow-competitors.

Brave the Elements
The Rules do not permit what's happening here. A player cannot be shielded from the elements in the act of making a stroke.
(R. 14-2)

A 1984 Rule change permits a Committee in charge of a team event to allow team captains or coaches to give advice, a privilege prohibited in the past. Now, for example, if the Committee so authorizes, a college or high school coach can stand on the tee of a par-3 hole and tell his team members what clubs have been used on the hole earlier and by whom.

However, this is not allowable if the tournament honors an individual winner as well as the winning team.

The USGA has been forced to split some fine hairs in interpreting "advice." Asking an opponent or fellow-competitor to name the club he has used is forbidden, but it's not a violation if you *look* into his bag to discover which club is missing. On the other hand, if your opponent or fellow-competitor should go to the extreme of draping a towel over his clubs to maintain secrecy, you are not allowed to strip the towel. A Decision says so. (As a practical matter, if I'm close to another player, I can identify the club he's selected by the club face angle 90 percent of the time.)

The Rulesmakers also had to agonize over the modern vogue for playing the game by yardage numbers. I know how far from the hole I am before I play almost every shot, and I also know the location of the hole on the green, which is expressed, for example, as six paces from the front and five paces from the right on a chart produced by tour officials and distributed at the first tee on each day of a tournament.

Given this availability of precise yardage data, what should happen under the Rules when a player asks another about yardage or the location of the hole, whether or not printed charts are available? Is that asking for "advice" or isn't it? The USGA has taken what seems to me the very pragmatic and sensible stand that distance from a tree, bunker or sprinkler head to the middle of the green is an ascertainable fact, that the location of the hole is a matter of "public information" and that neither comes under the heading of "counsel or suggestion," which are defined as "advice."

A piece of obscure but interesting history: The practice of charting courses by yards in terms of reference points ("123 yards from front of fairway bunker on right to middle of green") was the product of the nimble mind of Gene Andrews, a first-class amateur from Southern California who won both the USGA Public Links and Senior Amateur Championships. Andrews first charted a treeless links course in Great Britain during a practice round before a 1950s British Amateur Championship because he found that the barren land allowed him no sense of distance. Andrews continued the practice at home. Deane Beman picked it up from Gene during the 1958 U.S. Amateur Championship and passed it along to his good friend Jack Nicklaus. It wasn't very long before the televised image of Nicklaus peering at his yardage notes in fairways aroused the curiosity, and mimicry, of golfers everywhere.

8-2. Indicating Line of Play

Rule 8-2a is simple enough. When you can't see what you're aiming at, anyone can help you out by indicating the line to the target. But before you play the stroke, your helper has to get off that line, although

Indicating Line of Play

My caddie, or for that matter anyone else, can show me the line (left) to the hole, but he isn't allowed to stand on or near the line while the stroke is being played. He's moved off the line in the picture at right. (R. 8-2)

the flagstick *can* be held aloft to indicate the position of the hole.

The line of play on a putting green, however, is sacrosanct. Rule 8-2b is commonly violated when caddies or partners touch the green itself with a club or flagstick while pointing to what they consider to be the line. (The line, by the way, is not necessarily a straight line from ball to hole. The slope of the ground must be considered in resolving any questions about defining the line.)

RULE 9

INFORMATION AS TO STROKES TAKEN

The number of strokes a player has taken shall include any penalty strokes incurred.

9-1
General

A player who has incurred a penalty shall inform his opponent as soon as practicable. If he fails to do so, he shall be deemed to have given wrong information, even though he was not aware that he had incurred a penalty.

An opponent is entitled to ascertain from the player, during the play of a hole, the number of strokes he has taken and, after play of a hole, the number of strokes taken on the hole just completed.

If during the play of a hole the player gives or is deemed to give wrong information as to the number of strokes taken, he shall incur no penalty if he corrects the mistake before his opponent has played his next stroke. If after play of a hole the player gives or is deemed to give wrong information as to the number of strokes taken on the hole just completed, he shall incur no penalty if he corrects his mistake before any player plays from the next teeing ground or, in the case of the last hole of the match, before all players leave the putting green. If the player fails so to correct the wrong information, *he shall lose the hole.*

9-2
Match Play

A competitor who has incurred a penalty should inform his marker as soon as practicable.

9-3
Stroke Play

Rule 9 doesn't cause a stir in stroke play, since it all comes out in the wash at the end of a round when we check our cards, hole by hole. Rule 9-3 says that in stroke play a competitor should tell his marker of any penalties as soon as possible, but the difference between the conditional "should" and the absolute "shall" means that a competitor whose ball moves after he's taken his stance and addressed it need not shout that doleful fact to his marker, fifty yards on the other side of the fairway.

In match play, however, opponents should know how they stand at all times. If your opponent lies 3 in a bunker near the green, and you lie 1 only 125 yards from the hole, your next stroke is likely to be properly cautious. But if you think he only lies 2 because you don't know he incurred a penalty stroke along the way, you might be misled into flirting with the bunker yourself.

The word "deemed" in Rule 9 gives some readers pause. In this context, it means that a failure to announce that you've incurred a penalty is not unlike being asked how many strokes you've taken and coming up with the wrong answer.

Note, by the way, that ignorance of the Rules is no excuse. Example: your opponent removes a leaf behind his ball in a bunker on the 9th hole, but you don't see that violation. The hole is then seemingly won by him. As you're strolling down the 10th fairway, he casually remarks that he was able to make a good bunker shot on the 9th because he moved a leaf. If you know what you're doing, you'll tell him that a leaf is a loose impediment which can't be removed from a hazard, and that by not revealing the violation (even though he didn't know there was a violation) he gave you wrong information. He therefore lost the 9th hole. Instead of being 1 down, you're now 1 up.

ORDER OF PLAY

ORDER OF PLAY

a. TEEING GROUND

The side entitled to play first from the <u>teeing ground</u> is said to have the "honor."

The side which shall have the honor at the first teeing ground shall be determined by the order of the draw. In the absence of a draw, the honor should be decided by lot.

The side which wins a hole shall take the honor at the next teeing ground. If a hole has been halved, the side which had the honor at the previous teeing ground shall retain it.

b. OTHER THAN ON TEEING GROUND

When the balls are in play, the ball farther from the hole shall be played first. If the balls are equidistant from the hole, the ball to be played first should be decided by lot.

Exception: Rule 30-3c (best-ball and four-ball match play).

c. PLAYING OUT OF TURN

If a player plays when his opponent should have played, the opponent may immediately require the player to abandon the ball so played and, without penalty, play a ball in correct order (see Rule 20-5).

a. TEEING GROUND

The competitor entitled to play first from the <u>teeing ground</u> is said to have the "honor."

The competitor who shall have the honor at the first teeing ground shall be determined by the order of the draw. In the absence of a draw, the honor should be decided by lot.

The competitor with the lowest score at a hole shall take the honor at the next teeing ground. The competitor with the second lowest score shall play next and so on. If two or more competitors have the same score at a hole, they shall play

53

from the next teeing ground in the same order as at the previous teeing ground.

b. OTHER THAN ON TEEING GROUND

When the balls are in play, the ball farthest from the hole shall be played first. If two or more balls are equidistant from the hole, the ball to be played first should be decided by lot.

Exceptions: Rules 22 (ball interfering with or assisting play) and 31-5 (four-ball stroke play).

c. PLAYING OUT OF TURN

If a competitor plays out of turn, no penalty shall be incurred and the ball shall be played as it lies. If, however, the Committee determines that competitors have agreed to play in an order other than that set forth in Clauses 2a and 2b of this Rule to give one of them an advantage, *they shall be disqualified.*

(Incorrect order of play in threesomes and foursomes stroke play—see Rule 29-3.)

10-3
Provisional Ball or Second Ball from Teeing Ground

If a player plays a <u>provisional ball</u> or a second ball from a <u>teeing ground</u>, he should do so after his opponent or fellow-competitor has played his first <u>stroke</u>. If a player plays a provisional ball or a second ball out of turn, Clauses 1c and 2c of this Rule shall apply.

10-4
Ball Moved in Measuring

If a ball is moved in measuring to determine which ball is farther from the hole, no penalty is incurred and the ball shall be replaced.

The principle expressed in Rule 10 is that the ball farther from the hole shall be played first. Here's a summary of what happens when a ball is played out of turn in the two most common forms of play:

• Match play: The opponent may immediately require the player to replay the stroke. If played from the tee, the ball may be re-teed; if played through the green or from a hazard, the ball to be replayed is dropped; if played on a putting green, the ball is replaced. No penalty. This now applies to both an individual match and a four-ball match.

• Stroke play: No penalty, and the ball is played as it lies—not played over. However, if there's a conspiracy in order to circumvent the Rule in order to give one player an advantage, the players involved are to be disqualified. One example would occur on a par-3 hole played in a heavy wind if a player tries to help a friend by playing out of turn so the friend can gauge the effect of the wind on his ball.

Everyday golf is played on a handicap basis and the honor is determined by the net scores of the preceding hole.

One of my favorite golf stories turns on a question of "honor." According to Joe Dey, the USGA granted a special exemption from qualifying for the 1941 U.S. Open to one Dr. Walter Ratto of Brazil for reasons that are still obscure. Dr. Ratto stepped to the first tee of the Colonial Country Club at Fort Worth and slammed his ball into a tree very near the tee. The ball caromed behind the tee. The young American pro with whom Dr. Ratto was paired then asked the doctor, "Is it now my honor or are you away?" Answer: The pro should have driven.

Nudged Off the Tee
There's no penalty when a ball falls or is knocked off a tee before a stroke. The ball may be teed again. Remember, there can be no stroke without intent. (R. 11-2)

TEEING GROUND

RULE 11

TEEING GROUND

Definition

The ''teeing ground'' is the starting place for the hole to be played. It is a rectangular area two club-lengths in depth, the front and the sides of which are defined by the outside limits of two tee-markers. A ball is outside the teeing ground when all of it lies outside the teeing ground.

11-1
Teeing

In teeing, the ball may be placed on the ground, on an irregularity of surface created by the player on the ground or on a tee, sand or other substance in order to raise it off the ground.

A player may stand outside the <u>teeing ground</u> to play a ball within it.

When the first <u>stroke</u> with any ball (including a <u>provisional ball</u>) is played from the teeing ground, the tee-markers are immovable <u>obstructions</u> (see Rule 24-2).

11-2
Ball Falling off Tee

If a ball, when not <u>in play</u>, falls off a tee or is knocked off a tee by the player in addressing it, it may be re-teed without penalty, but if a <u>stroke</u> is made at the ball in these circumstances, whether the ball is moving or not, the stroke shall be counted but no penalty shall be incurred.

11-3
Playing Outside Teeing Ground

a. MATCH PLAY
If a player, when starting a hole, plays a ball from outside the <u>teeing ground</u>, the opponent may immediately require the player to replay the stroke from within the teeing ground, without penalty.

b. STROKE PLAY
If a competitor, when starting a hole, plays a ball from outside the <u>teeing ground</u>, *he shall be penalized two strokes and*

shall then play a ball from within the teeing ground. Strokes played by a competitor from outside the teeing ground do not count in his score. If the competitor fails to rectify his mistake before making a <u>stroke</u> on the next teeing ground or, in the case of the last hole of the round, before leaving the <u>putting green</u>, *he shall be disqualified.*

11-1. Teeing

Historical note: The wooden tee was not invented until the turn of the century and didn't come into common use until the 1920s. Before then, balls were commonly teed on tiny pyramids of wet sand, which was usually stored in buckets near each tee.

11-2. Ball Falling off Tee

Whenever a ball falls off or is nudged accidentally from a tee, some joker has to say "That's one." It is not, because the definition of a stroke told us that there is no stroke unless the club moves forward and the player *intends* to strike the ball. The ball is not in play until a stroke is made. Rule 11-2 is necessary only to resolve the question of whether or not the ball can be teed again—and of course it can.

● The atmosphere must have been electric in a club match reported by a Massachusetts golfer. It led to a decision which goes like this: A teed her ball, addressed it and then missed it completely. A whiff! Then, after addressing the ball again, A nudged her ball from the tee. B said A was then shooting 3 and must play the ball where it lay even though it was still within the teeing ground. A vehemently claimed she could re-tee without penalty.

Answer: Poor A did lie 2. The whiff was one stroke. According to a Definition, A's ball was in play as soon as she made a stroke on the teeing ground. Therefore A's ball was in play as soon as she whiffed it and it was also in play when she accidentally moved it. Since she moved it after address, she incurred a one-stroke penalty and had to play the ball as it lay, as required by Rule 18-2b.

I can't help but remember John Mahaffey completing his stroke as his ball was toppling from the tee on a hole at the Firestone Country Club. John's driver barely made contact with the ball, which dribbled only a few yards off the tee and into a rotten lie. John, whose sense of humor is one of the tour's redeeming features, later lamented what terrible luck he'd suffered in not missing the ball entirely so that it still would have been teed up.

11-3. Playing Outside Teeing Ground

I've never known an instance when a golfer purposely teed his ball in front of the tee-markers, but it does happen occasionally and usually because the markers have been installed so carelessly that a line drawn between the front of the markers would not form a right angle with the line of play.

A ball teed outside the teeing ground raises a nice question of ethics. In match play the opponent of the player whose ball is teed in the wrong place has every opportunity to use the Rules cruelly by requiring the shot to be replayed. That's not the way the game should be played. If I saw an opponent's ball teed ahead of the markers, I'd let him know about it and I'd expect him to do the same for me.

Playing from outside the teeing ground in stroke play calls for a two-stroke penalty. Failure to rectify the mistake before playing from the next tee results in disqualification. Suppose a player in stroke play plays from the wrong set of tee markers or is unfamiliar with the course and begins to play a hole out of sequence. Let's say he then plays a second stroke before the error is brought to his attention. Rule 11-3 says that he must return to the correct set of markers and play the hole correctly. The stroke he plays from the correct markers is his third (not fifth), since the strokes he played starting at the wrong markers do not count and only the penalty strokes are added.

PLAYING THE BALL

RULE 12

SEARCHING FOR AND IDENTIFYING BALL

Definitions

A "hazard" is any <u>bunker</u> or <u>water hazard</u>.

A "bunker" is a <u>hazard</u> consisting of a prepared area of ground, often a hollow, from which turf or soil has been removed and replaced with sand or the like. Grass-covered ground bordering or within a bunker is not part of the bunker.

A "water hazard" is any sea, lake, pond, river, ditch, surface drainage ditch or other open water course (whether or not containing water) and anything of a similar nature.

All ground or water within the margin of a water hazard is part of the water hazard. The margin of a water hazard is deemed to extend vertically upwards. Stakes and lines defining the margins of water hazards are in the hazards.

12-1

Searching for Ball; Seeing Ball

If a ball lies in long grass, rushes, bushes, whins, heather or the like, only so much thereof may be touched as will enable the player to find and identify his ball, except that nothing shall be done which improves its lie, the area of his intended swing or his line of play.

A player is not necessarily entitled to see his ball when playing a stroke.

In a <u>hazard</u>, if the ball is covered by <u>loose impediments</u> or sand, the player may remove only as much thereof as will enable him to see a part of the ball. If the ball is moved in such removal, no penalty is incurred and the ball shall be replaced. As to removal of loose impediments outside a hazard, see Rule 23.

If a ball lying in <u>casual water</u>, <u>ground under repair</u> or a hole, cast or runway made by a burrowing animal, a reptile or a bird is accidentally moved during search, no penalty is in-

59

Buried in Sand

My ball is completely buried in the sand of a bunker. All I'm allowed to do is brush aside enough sand so that I can see a piece of the ball— but no more. It doesn't matter if I can't identify the ball, since there's no penalty for playing a wrong ball in a hazard. (R. 12-1)

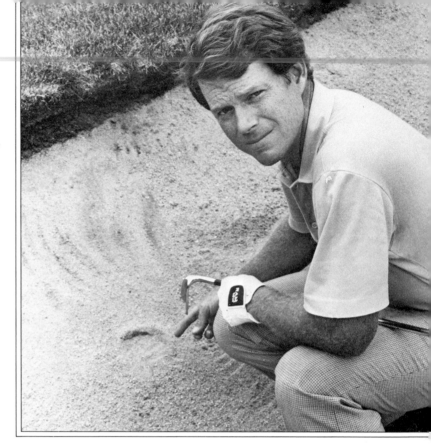

curred; the ball shall be replaced, unless the player elects to proceed under Rule 25-1b.

If a ball is believed to be lying in water in a <u>water hazard</u>, the player may probe for it with a club or otherwise. If the ball is moved in so doing, no penalty shall be incurred; the ball shall be replaced, unless the player elects to proceed under Rule 26-1.

PENALTY FOR BREACH OF RULE 12-1:
Match play—Loss of hole; Stroke play—Two strokes.

12-2
Identifying Ball

The responsibility for playing the proper ball rests with the player. Each player should put an identification mark on his ball.

Except in a <u>hazard</u>, the player may, without penalty, lift a ball he believes to be his own for the purpose of identification and clean it to the extent necessary for identification. If the ball is the player's ball, he shall replace it on the spot from which it was lifted. Before the player lifts the ball, he shall announce his intention to his opponent in match play or his marker or a fellow-competitor in stroke play and give his opponent, marker or fellow-competitor an opportunity to observe the lifting and replacement. If he lifts the ball without announcing his intention in advance or giving his opponent, marker or fellow-competitor an opportunity to observe, or if

he lifts his ball for identification in a hazard, *he shall incur a penalty of one stroke* and the ball shall be replaced.

If a player who is required to replace a ball fails to do so, *he shall incur the penalty* for a breach of Rule 20-3a, but no additional penalty under Rule 12-2 shall be applied.

12-1. Searching for Ball; Seeing Ball

One key point is that a player whose ball is in an awkward position can't use the excuse of either searching for the ball or identifying it in order to make the recovery shot easier.

Effective in 1984, a player who moves his ball while searching for it in casual water or ground under repair is not penalized.

12-2. Identifying Ball

A change introduced in 1984 alters the identification procedure. When a player isn't sure a ball is his, he must announce his intention to his opponent, marker or fellow-competitor, and give him the opportunity to observe the lifting and replacement. Incidentally, the position of the ball lifted must be marked—a requirement of Rule 20-1.

A ball lifted in this circumstance is *not* to be cleaned unless there's no other way to identify the ball, and then only enough to establish its identity.

The privilege of lifting for identification does not exist in hazards because there's no penalty for playing a wrong ball in a hazard.

RULE 13

BALL PLAYED AS IT LIES; AREA OF INTENDED SWING AND LINE OF PLAY; STANCE

Definitions

A "hazard" is any <u>bunker</u> or <u>water hazard</u>.

A "bunker" is a <u>hazard</u> consisting of a prepared area of ground, often a hollow, from which turf or soil has been removed and replaced with sand or the like. Grass-covered ground bordering or within a bunker is not part of the bunker.

A "water hazard" is any sea, lake, pond, river, ditch, surface drainage ditch or other open water course (whether or not containing water) and anything of a similar nature.

All ground or water within the margin of a water hazard is part of the water hazard. The margin of a water hazard is deemed to extend vertically upwards. Stakes and lines defining the margins of water hazards are in the hazards.

13-1
Ball Played As It Lies

The ball shall be played as it lies, except as otherwise provided in the Rules. (Ball at rest moved—Rule 18.)

13-2
Improving Lie, Area of Intended Swing or Line of Play

Except as provided in the Rules, a player shall not improve or allow to be improved:

the position or lie of his ball,

the area of his intended swing or

his line of play

by any of the following actions:

moving, bending or breaking anything growing or fixed

Don't Improve the Lie
Here's an example of a blatant violation. The lie is being improved by pressing down behind the ball so that it sits up better. One of the underlying principles behind the Rules of Golf is that you play the ball as it lies. (R. 13-2)

(including objects defining <u>out of bounds</u>) or

 removing or pressing down sand, loose soil, replaced divots, other cut turf placed in position or other irregularities of surface

except as follows:

 as may occur in fairly taking his <u>stance</u>,

 in making a <u>stroke</u> or the backward movement of his club for a stroke,

 on the <u>teeing ground</u> in creating or eliminating irregularities of surface, or

 on the <u>putting green</u> in removing sand and loose soil as provided in Rule 16-1a or in repairing damage as provided in Rule 16-1c.

The club may be grounded only lightly and shall not be pressed on the ground.

Exception: Ball lying in or touching hazard—Rule 13-4.

A player is entitled to place his feet firmly in taking his stance, but he shall not build a stance.

13-3
Building Stance

13-4
Ball Lying in or Touching Hazard

Except as provided in the Rules, before making a <u>stroke</u> at a ball which lies in or touches a <u>hazard</u> (whether a <u>bunker</u> or a <u>water hazard</u>), the player shall not:

 a. Test the condition of the hazard or any similar hazard,

 b. Touch the ground in the hazard or water in the water hazard with a club or otherwise, or

 c. Touch or move a <u>loose impediment</u> lying in or touching the hazard.

Exceptions:

1. At address or in the backward movement for the stroke, the club may touch any <u>obstruction</u> or any grass, bush, tree or other growing thing.

2. The player may place his clubs in a <u>hazard</u>, provided nothing is done which may constitute testing the soil or improving the lie of the ball.

3. The player after playing the stroke, or his <u>caddie</u> at any time without the authority of the player, may smooth sand or soil in the hazard, provided that, if the ball still lies in the hazard, nothing is done which improves the lie of the ball or assists the player in his subsequent play of the hole.

PENALTY FOR BREACH OF RULE:

Match play—Loss of hole; Stroke play—Two strokes.

(Searching for ball—Rule 12-1.)

It may well be that Rule 13 is violated more often than any other Rule. The impulse to make the stroke a little bit easier by moving anything bothersome or by pressing down with the clubhead is powerful. Moreover, the application of this Rule often involves judgment rather than agreed-upon facts. This Rule is violated:

• When, during a practice swing, a branch or twig is snapped or leaves are removed, making the actual stroke easier to accomplish.

Touching a Hazard

Before you play a stroke in a hazard the ground (or, in a water hazard, the water) may not be touched. When a ball lies in a hazard, it is addressed as soon as the player takes a stance. If the club touches the sand during the backswing, there's a violation. (R. 13-4)

Grass in a Hazard
When a ball is playable in a water hazard it's often surrounded by tall grass. In the act of addressing the ball, I'm permitted to touch the grass, but it would be a violation to ground the club. (R. 13-4)

• When a player brushes aside sand or loose soil on his line that is not on a putting green.

• When a ball lies in shrubbery and the player gets to the ball like a bull in a china shop by breaking, bending or moving branches that bother the stroke or were in his line and which he need not have disturbed in order to take a fair stance.

The R&A and USGA say this about the knocking down of leaves during a practice swing: "Whether a player who knocks leaves down with a practice swing is in breach of this Rule depends on the circumstances. In some cases the knocking down of a number of leaves would not improve the area of the intended swing, in which case there would be no breach of the Rules. In other cases, the knocking down

65

of one large leaf might improve the area of the intended swing, in which case there would be a breach."

There was a famous violation of Rule 13-2 during the 1982 Tournament of Champions. Ron Streck, the leader, was inhibited by the branches of an evergreen tree as he addressed his ball. They obscured his vision. Ron braided the offending branches, which were right where he wanted his head to be. He had no idea he was wrong. But plenty of television viewers did. Their calls resulted in a review of the videotape before Ron completed his round. A two-stroke penalty was assessed.

TV viewers thought Andy Bean broke the same rule during the 1982 Doral Tournament. Andy had knocked down a few leaves while practicing how to play a recovery shot next to a tree. It was ruled, and properly so, that the dislodging of those leaves did not assist him. Bean went on to win the tournament.

The words "line of play" seem to cry out for clarification. Hence this Decision explaining the term "line of play" in Rules 8-2, 13-2, 23-1 and 24-1: "The line of play is the direction which the player wishes his ball to take after a stroke plus a reasonable distance on either side of the intended direction and beyond the intended objective. The line of play is both in the air and on the ground."

Here's another "line of play" Decision: "There is a bunker between A's ball and the hole. Before playing, A smooths footprints and other irregularities in the bunker on his line of play. Was A in breach of Rule 13-2?"

"Yes, such action would improve the line of play, contrary to Rule 13-2."

As for Rule 13-3, an extreme example of "building a stance" would be to climb on a golf-cart seat to flail away at a ball lodged in a tree. A more common violation occurs when players, faced with taking an uneven stance in a bunker, pound down the side of a bunker with their heels in order to get their feet level.

I've always been puzzled by the seeming contradiction in the Rules prohibiting me from testing the condition of a hazard in Rule 13-4 but allowing me, on the other hand, to take a firm stance in Rule 13-3. The USGA once wrestled with this contradiction before saying: "Obviously, there is a gray area between the two clauses. The gray area is a necessary evil inasmuch as it would be unfair to prohibit a player from taking a firm stance when his ball lies in the sand. Whether a player infringes on this gray area to his own advantage is often a matter which can be controlled only by his own conscience."

Some keys to the use of Rule 13-4:

● Remember that when your ball lies in a hazard you may not move loose impediments in the hazard, and that loose impediments include stones and leaves. If you so much as brush one with your club during your backswing (which is before the stroke), you violate the Rule. Accidentally moving a loose impediment, provided it is not moved in making the backswing and does not improve the lie or the area of the intended swing, is not a violation.

● On the other hand, you are permitted to move movable obstructions—man-made objects, such as bottles, candy wrappers and cigarette butts.

Ball Marks and Line of Play

You may repair a ball mark on the putting green (left) even though your ball is off the putting green. But the right to repair ball marks is strictly limited to the putting green, so you may not repair a mark on your line on an apron (right) even though you intend to putt. The apron is not part of the putting green. After making the stroke, though, you should repair the damage as part of the game's Etiquette.

RULE 14

STRIKING THE BALL

Definition

A "stroke" is the forward movement of the club made with the intention of fairly striking at and moving the ball.

14-1
Ball to Be Fairly Struck At

The ball shall be fairly struck at with the head of the club and must not be pushed, scraped or spooned.

14-2
Assistance

In making a stroke, a player shall not accept physical assistance or protection from the elements.

PENALTY FOR BREACH OF RULE 14-1 OR -2:
Match play—Loss of hole; Stroke play—Two strokes.

14-3
Artificial Devices and Unusual Equipment

Except as provided in the Rules, during a stipulated round the player shall not use any artificial device or unusual equipment:

a. For the purpose of gauging or measuring distance or conditions which might affect his play; or

b. Which might assist him in gripping the club, in making a stroke or in his play, except that plain gloves may be worn, resin, tape or gauze may be applied to the grip (provided such application does not render the grip non-conforming under Rule 4-1c) and a towel or handkerchief may be wrapped around the grip.

PENALTY FOR BREACH OF RULE 14-3: *Disqualification.*

14-4
Striking the Ball More than Once

If a player's club strikes the ball more than once in the course of a <u>stroke</u>, the player shall count the stroke and *add a penalty stroke,* making two strokes in all.

14-5
Playing Moving Ball

A player shall not play while his ball is moving.
Exceptions:
Ball falling off tee—Rule 11-2.
Striking the ball more than once—Rule 14-4.
Ball moving in water—Rule 14-6.

When the ball begins to move only after the player has begun the <u>stroke</u> or the backward movement of his club for the stroke, he shall incur no penalty under this Rule for playing a moving ball, but he is not exempt from any penalty incurred under the following Rules:
Ball at rest moved by player—Rule 18-2a.
Ball at rest moving after address—Rule 18-2b.
Ball at rest moving after loose impediment touched—Rule 18-2c.

When a ball is moving in water in a <u>water hazard</u>, the player may, without penalty, make a <u>stroke</u>, but he must not delay making his stroke in order to allow the wind or current to improve the position of the ball. A ball moving in water in a water hazard may be lifted if the player elects to invoke Rule 26.

PENALTY FOR BREACH OF RULE 14-5 OR -6:
Match play—Loss of hole; Stroke play—Two strokes.

14-6
Ball Moving in Water

14-1. Ball to Be Fairly Struck At

The critical, if sometimes hard-to-determine difference between a genuine stroke and a push was dealt with in this Decision: "A player's ball lies close to an out-of-bounds fence, but there is room behind the ball to insert an iron club or a putter and leave a space of half an inch between the ball and the face of the club. If the player plays a stroke with such a limited backswing, is he in breach of Rule 14-1?"

"It is possible to strike a ball fairly with a half-inch backswing. However, in most cases the player would be pushing the ball, contrary to Rule 14-1. In the absence of strong evidence to the contrary, it should be ruled that the player has pushed the ball.

"In order to strike the ball fairly, it must be swung at with the clubhead. If the ball is moved by any other method, it has been pushed, scraped or spooned.

"If a ball is fairly struck at, there is only momentary contact between the clubhead and the ball or whatever intervenes between the clubhead and the ball."

14-2. Assistance

As for Rule 14-2, the only physical assistance I can imagine would be to have someone hold me steady as I took a precarious stance on a steep slope. Even your caddie is not allowed to hold on to you. Protection against the elements, however, is something we could all use when a high wind causes rain to slant. Without this restriction you'd see caddies shielding their players from the elements with huge umbrellas.

14-3. Artificial Devices and Unusual Equipment

The best way to illustrate Rule 14-3 about artificial devices is to present a series of examples.

Not artificial devices. Using weighted head covers; wearing regular eyeglasses; dropping a handkerchief to determine wind conditions; applying gauze tape or wrapping a handkerchief around the grip to keep from slipping; using a booklet illustrating distances to holes from various landmarks; using a hand warmer, provided it is not also used to affect the temperature of golf balls.

Artificial devices. Using any of the following: field glasses which have a range-finder feature; an actual plumb line—a weight suspended from a string; a ball warmer during a round; an electronic instrument used to find balls which have transmitters embedded in their cores.

14-4. Striking the Ball More than Once

I have had my problems with Rule 14-4. During the 1977 Memorial Tournament at Jack Nicklaus' Muirfield Golf Club, I tried to putt my ball out of heavy grass. When I struck the ball it tangled in the grass and I hit it again in a continuation of the same stroke. I immediately —and sorrowfully—called the penalty on myself.

And during the 1983 PGA Championship at Riviera, on the second hole of the first round, I made the mistake of trying to play a delicate little shot left-handed from up against a tree. I hit the ball twice and ended up with a fat 7 on a par-4 hole.

14-5. Playing a Moving Ball

Frankly, I've never been able to figure out why it's necessary to have a Rule prohibiting play while a ball is moving, but now I think I understand it. Suppose your ball is at rest, poised delicately on a slope, and as you approach the ball it begins to roll—toward a water hazard or a boundary. It might be to your advantage to swat at it on the run—but that turns the game into a form of field hockey.

Golfers are often thrown for a loop by one provision of Rule 14-5. According to Rule 18-2b, if your ball moves once you've addressed it (taken your stance and, through the green, grounded your club), you are deemed to have caused it to move. Okay, suppose you lie 2 in the rough, and after you've addressed the ball and begun your stroke, your ball moves. You complete the stroke and hit the ball. Rule 14-5 says you are not exempted from Rule 18-2b; you therefore incur a one-stroke penalty and now lie 4.

14-6. Ball Moving in Water

The Rules do allow for play of a moving ball in water. If a ball is playable in water, it's often difficult to tell whether the ball is moving or not. Thus it seems only right that the player should be allowed a crack at it, moving or not. The most celebrated instance of playing a moving ball took place before I was born, during the 1938 U.S. Open at the Cherry Hills Country Club near Denver. Pro Ray Ainsley put his second shot into a creek on the par-4 16th hole and decided the ball was playable. Ainsley made fourteen strokes at the ball in the hazard. Sometimes the ball was moving when he made a stroke and sometimes it wasn't. In any event, he holed out in nineteen—the most strokes ever taken on one hole in our Open.

RULE 15

PLAYING A WRONG BALL

Definition

A "wrong ball" is any ball other than:
  a. The ball in play,
  b. A provisional ball or
  c. In stroke play, a second ball played under Rule 3-3 or Rule 20-7b.

A player must hole out with the ball played from the <u>teeing ground</u> unless a Rule permits him to substitute another ball.

15-1
General

If a player plays a stroke with a <u>wrong ball</u> except in a <u>hazard</u>, *he shall lose the hole.*

If a player plays any strokes in a hazard with a wrong ball, there is no penalty. Strokes played in a hazard with a wrong ball do not count in the player's score.

If the player and opponent exchange balls during the play of a hole, the first to play the wrong ball other than from a hazard shall lose the hole; when this cannot be determined, the hole shall be played out with the balls exchanged.

15-2
Match Play

If a competitor plays a stroke with a <u>wrong ball</u> except in a <u>hazard</u>, *he shall add two penalty strokes to his score* and shall then play the correct ball.

If a competitor plays any strokes in a hazard with a wrong ball, there is no penalty.

Strokes played with a wrong ball do not count in a competitor's score.

If a competitor holes out with a wrong ball, but has not made a stroke on the next <u>teeing ground</u> or, in the case of the last hole of the round, has not left the <u>putting green</u>, he may rectify his mistake by playing the correct ball, subject to the prescribed penalty. *The competitor shall be disqualified* if he does not so rectify his mistake.

Note: *For procedure to be followed by owner of wrong ball, see Rule 18-1.*

15-3
Stroke Play

The first two sections of Rule 15 are straightforward and simple, but the third section, for stroke play, is just plain tricky and onerous. Let's tackle them in order:

General: You may not substitute balls during a hole unless specifically authorized to do so by the Rules. This precludes the use of what some golfers call "putting balls," the shiny and unscarred ones they would like to use after risking a battered veteran off the tee on a water hole.

Match Play: As soon as a player plays a wrong ball, except in a hazard, he loses the hole; in four-ball play the errant player is disqualified for that hole but there's no penalty for his partner, even if the wrong ball belonged to his partner.

Stroke Play: When a competitor plays a wrong ball, except in a hazard, he immediately suffers a two-stroke penalty and doesn't count any strokes played with the wrong ball. Moreover, if the mistake is not rectified, the penalty is disqualification. (Rectification means returning to play the correct ball before teeing off on the next hole or, if the mistake is made on the last hole, before he leaves the putting green.)

I've played a wrong ball only once in my professional career. During the pro tour's 1972 Team Championship (four-ball stroke play) at the Laurel Valley Golf Club in Ligonier, Pennsylvania, my partner was Bob Zender. We both pushed our drives to the right on a par-4 and managed to play each other's ball. We discovered the errors before either of us had played a third stroke. It meant two-stroke penalties for both of us and we had to go back and play correctly. I "birdied" the hole with the correct ball, but our score for the hole was a bogie 5.

Some Rule 15 Decisions to chew on:

• A player swings at a ball, misses and then discovers it wasn't his ball.

Answer: In match play the player made a stroke at a wrong ball and lost the hole; in stroke play he incurred a two-stroke penalty.

• "In stroke play, a competitor considered his ball lost in a water hazard, although there was not reasonable evidence to that effect. He dropped a ball behind the hazard under Rule 26-1b and played it. A fellow-competitor then questioned the competitor's procedure. What is the ruling?"

"The ball dropped behind the hazard was not substituted under an applicable Rule and thus it was not the ball in play but rather a wrong ball (Rule 15-3)—see Definitions of 'Ball in Play' and 'Wrong Ball.' The competitor incurred a penalty of two strokes for playing the ball dropped behind the hazard and he must abandon it and, if the original ball is not found within five minutes, proceed under Rule 27-1."

• A player in stroke play doesn't realize his ball is out of bounds and plays a stroke from OB.

Answer: The player played a wrong ball, since the ball was no longer in play once it went out of bounds. He must rectify his error before playing from the next tee or be disqualified.

THE PUTTING GREEN

RULE 16

THE PUTTING GREEN

Definitions

The "putting green" is all ground of the hole being played which is specially prepared for putting or otherwise defined as such by the Committee. A ball is on the putting green when any part of it touches the putting green.

A ball is "holed" when it is at rest within the circumference of the hole and all of it is below the level of the lip of the hole.

16-1
General

a. TOUCHING LINE OF PUTT

The line of putt must not be touched except:

(i) the player may move sand, loose soil and other loose impediments by picking them up or by brushing them aside with his hand or a club without pressing anything down;

(ii) in addressing the ball, the player may place the club in front of the ball without pressing anything down;

(iii) in measuring—Rule 10-4;

(iv) in lifting the ball—Rule 16-1b;

(v) in repairing old hole plugs or ball marks—Rule 16-1c; and

(vi) in removing movable obstructions—Rule 24-1.

(Indicating line for putting on putting green—Rule 8-2b.)

b. LIFTING BALL

A ball on the <u>putting green</u> may be lifted and, if desired, cleaned. A ball so lifted shall be replaced on the spot from which it was lifted.

c. REPAIR OF HOLE PLUGS AND BALL MARKS

The player may repair an old hole plug or damage to the <u>putting green</u> caused by the impact of a ball, whether or not the player's ball lies on the putting green. If the ball is moved in the process of such repair, it shall be replaced, without penalty.

73

Don't Repair Spike Marks
The line of putt is sacrosanct. It is not to be improved unless the Rules specify exceptions —for example, repairing ball marks and removing loose impediments. This most assuredly means that irregularities on the line of putt, such as raised tufts of grass, may not be tamped down, as is being done here. (R. 16-1a)

Don't Use a Hat as a Brush
You are allowed to pick up or brush aside loose impediments on the line of putt. But all you can use are your hands or a club. If anything else is used—a hat, for instance—it's a violation.

Repairing Ball Marks

Ball marks on putting greens may be repaired, even if they're on your line. As a matter of fact, they should be repaired, no matter where they are. I use a tee to loosen the soil around the mark. After the compacted soil has been loosened at several positions, I pull the turf toward the center of the damaged spot. The smoothing process can be done either with a putter or by stepping down on the spot. (R. 16-1c)

d. Testing Surface

During the play of a hole, a player shall not test the surface of the putting green by rolling a ball or roughening or scraping the surface.

e. Standing Astride or on Line of Putt

The player shall not make a stroke on the putting green from a stance astride, or with either foot touching, the line of the putt or an extension of that line behind the ball. For the purpose of this Clause only, the line of putt does not extend beyond the hole.

f. Position of Caddie or Partner

While making the stroke, the player shall not allow his caddie, his partner or his partner's caddie to position himself on or close to an extension of the line of putt behind the ball.

g. Other Ball to Be at Rest

A player shall not play a stroke or touch his ball in play while another ball is in motion after a stroke on the putting green.

h. Ball Overhanging Hole

When any part of the ball overhangs the edge of the hole, the player is allowed enough time to reach the hole without unreasonable delay and an additional 10 seconds to determine whether the ball is at rest. If by then the ball has not fallen into the hole, it is deemed to be at rest.

PENALTY FOR BREACH OF RULE 16-1:
Match play—Loss of hole; Stroke play—Two strokes.

16-2
Conceding Opponent's Next Stroke

When the opponent's ball is at rest or is deemed to be at rest, the player may concede the opponent to have holed out with his next stroke and the ball may be removed by either side with a club or otherwise.

A disproportionate number of Rules incidents occur on putting greens, where all players and balls eventually converge. One of the happiest consequences of the reorganization of the Rules of Golf in 1984 is a vastly simplified presentation of the complexities of life on putting greens.

16-1a. Touching Line of Putt

The line of putt is holy ground. It is not to be touched except during the six activities specified in 16-1a.

Here are some transgressions:

• Repairing spike or scuff marks, which would be so difficult to define for Rules purposes that a Rule permitting their repair could open the door for repair of any minor imperfections in the putting surface. It would also make the game slower, and we surely don't need that.

• Brushing aside or sopping up casual water. The same goes for dew.

• Walking or stepping on the line of putt, if the line is improved. The R&A ruled in 1969 that walking on the line is okay if it's done accidentally *and* the line is not improved.

Direction for Putting

My caddie or my partner can use the flagstick to point to the line of putt. But if he touches the putting green in front of, to the side of, or behind the hole, I'm penalized.

• Brushing away leaves with a hat or towel. All you can use are your hands or a club.

16-1b. Lifting Ball

The Rules used to imply that the ball had to be cleaned when it was lifted on a green. Not any more. Personally, I think the average golfer indulges in lifting and cleaning too much! We need to speed up the game.

16-1c. Repair of Hole Plugs and Ball Marks

Everyone should acquire the habit of scanning for ball marks to repair, no matter who made them.

16-1d. Testing Surface

If I could rub the surface of greens, it would help me to "read" the grain better and make putting a little easier. Putting should remain a craft that requires exquisite sensitivity.

Golfers should avoid cleaning balls by rubbing them on greens, notwithstanding a Decision that says cleaning the ball by rubbing it on the surface of the putting green does not violate the Rules, provided the act is not for the purpose of testing the surface of the green. The Decision recommends that the ball be cleaned in another manner so as to eliminate questions as to the player's intentions.

16-1e. Standing Astride or on Line of Putt

This clause bars what used to be called "straddle" putting, a variation popularized by Sam Snead. Sam's reaction was to continue to putt croquet-style, but to stand with both feet together *off* an extension of the line of putt, behind the ball.

16-1f. Position of Caddie or Partner

There was a time when prominent players, Johnny Miller foremost among them, had their caddies crouch behind them to give counsel on alignment. It was stopped by the Rules-makers, who argued that the practice was making the caddie into something more than he should be.

Partners in four-ball events should be aware of this clause, since it applies to them as well.

16-1g. Other Ball to Be at Rest

That's easy. No one plays or touches his ball while another ball is in motion.

16-1h. Ball Overhanging Hole

The code used to refer to a "few" seconds. Now it specifies that the player is allowed enough time to reach the hole without unreasonable delay, plus ten seconds.

These are a couple of obvious ramifications in match play:

• If a player's ball is overhanging the hole, he's entitled to his ten seconds. Should an opponent concede the next stroke before ten seconds by knocking the ball away, the opponent has infringed the player's right and loses the hole.

● After ten seconds, the player may no longer insist the ball is moving. In match play, his opponent may then concede the putt.

16-2. Conceding Opponent's Next Stroke

Concessions should be loud and clear. Once a putt is conceded, that's it. The player is considered to have holed out on his next stroke. The concession may not be recalled or declined. (If the player nonetheless putts and misses, it is irrelevant.) In four-ball match play, if a putt has been conceded but the player goes ahead and putts anyway because he hopes to show his partner the correct line, the *partner* should be disqualified from that hole, since he was the intended beneficiary of the act.

RULE 17

THE FLAGSTICK

Before and during the stroke, the player may have the flagstick attended, removed or held up to indicate the position of the hole. This may be done only on the authority of the player before he plays his stroke.

If the flagstick is attended or removed by an opponent, a fellow-competitor or the caddie of either with the player's knowledge and no objection is made, the player shall be deemed to have authorized it. If a player or a caddie attends or removes the flagstick or stands near the hole while a

17-1
Flagstick Attended, Removed or Held Up

Flagstick Held Aloft
When a green is elevated, it isn't always possible to see the flagstick when you address the ball. In that case, the flagstick may be held up at the hole (1), and it can be attended in that manner during the stroke. But if the flagstick is held aloft away from the hole (2), the caddie has to get off the line before the stroke is played.

stroke is being played, he shall be deemed to attend the flag-stick until the ball comes to rest.

If the flagstick is not attended before the stroke is played, it shall not be attended or removed while the ball is in motion.

17-2
Unauthorized Attendance

a. MATCH PLAY

In match play, an opponent or his caddie shall not attend or remove the flagstick without the player's knowledge or authority.

b. STROKE PLAY

In stroke play, if a fellow-competitor or his caddie attends or removes the flagstick without the competitor's knowledge or authority while the competitor is making a stroke or his ball is in motion, *the fellow-competitor shall incur the penalty* for breach of this Rule. In such circumstances, if the competitor's ball strikes the flagstick or the person attending it, the competitor incurs no penalty and the ball shall be played as it lies, except that, if the stroke was played from the putting green, the stroke shall be replayed.

PENALTY FOR BREACH OF RULE 17-1 OR -2:
Match play—Loss of hole; Stroke play—Two strokes.

17-3
Ball Striking Flagstick or Attendant

The player's ball shall not strike:

a. The flagstick when attended or removed by the player, his partner or either of their caddies, or by another person with the player's knowledge or authority; or

b. The player's caddie, his partner or his partner's caddie when attending the flagstick, or another person attending the flagstick with the player's knowledge or authority, or equipment carried by any such person; or

c. The flagstick in the hole, unattended, when the ball has been played from the putting green.

PENALTY FOR BREACH OF RULE 17-3:
Match play—Loss of hole; Stroke play—Two strokes, and the ball shall be played as it lies.

17-4
Ball Resting Against Flagstick

If the ball rests against the flagstick when it is in the hole, the player or someone authorized by him may move or remove the flagstick and if the ball falls into the hole, the player shall be deemed to have holed out at his last stroke; otherwise, the ball, if moved, shall be placed on the lip of the hole, without penalty.

The flagstick exists in order to indicate the location of the hole. Its incidental use as a backstop has been a subject of controversy and the cause of many Rules changes over the years. Now, happily, the Rule has settled into a form we can all understand:

• If your ball is *on* the putting green and it strikes the flagstick, whether it's attended or unattended, the penalty is loss of hole in match play and two strokes in stroke play.

• If your ball is *off* the green, you may use the flagstick as a backstop. There is no penalty for striking it as long as it is not attended.

Striking the Flagstick
When I putt from off the green, I may prefer to have the flagstick remain in the hole, since there's no penalty for striking the flagstick from off the green. But when the ball is played from on the green, there is a penalty for striking the flagstick, which should either be attended or set aside. (R. 17-3)

81

Stop That Outside Agency!
The player is Johnny Bulla;
the scene the 1950 U.S. Open
Championship at the Merion
Golf Club. An outside agency
snatched Bulla's ball and
made a clean getaway.
Whenever an outside agency
—be it human, animal or
mechanical—moves a ball,
the ball is to be replaced
without penalty. If the outside
agency is a successful thief,
another ball may be
substituted. (R. 18-1)

BALL MOVED, DEFLECTED OR STOPPED

BALL AT REST MOVED

A ball is deemed to have "moved" if it leaves its position and comes to rest in any other place.

An "outside agency" is any agency not part of the match or, in stroke play, not part of a competitor's side, and includes a referee, a marker, an observer or a forecaddie. Neither wind nor water is an outside agency.

"Equipment" is anything used, worn or carried by or for the player except any ball he has played and any small object, such as a coin or a tee, when used to mark the position of a ball or the extent of an area in which a ball is to be dropped. Equipment includes a golf cart, whether or not motorized. If such a cart is shared by more than one player, its status under the Rules is the same as that of a caddie employed by more than one player. See "Caddie."

A player has "addressed the ball" when he has taken his stance and has also grounded his club, except that in a hazard a player has addressed the ball when he has taken his stance.

Taking the "stance" consists in a player placing his feet in position for and preparatory to making a stroke.

Definitions

If a ball at rest is moved by an outside agency, the player shall incur no penalty and the ball shall be replaced before the player plays another stroke. If the ball moved is not im-

18-1

By Outside Agency   83

mediately recoverable, another ball may be substituted.

(Player's ball at rest moved by another ball—see Rule 18-5.)

18-2
By Player, Partner, Caddie or Equipment

a. GENERAL

When a player's ball is in play, if:

(i) the player, his partner or either of their caddies lifts or moves it, touches it purposely (except with a club in the act of addressing it) or causes it to move except as permitted by a Rule, or

(ii) equipment of the player or his partner causes the ball to move,

the player shall incur a penalty stroke. The ball shall be replaced unless the movement of the ball occurs after the player has begun his swing and he does not discontinue his swing.

Under the Rules no penalty is incurred if a player accidentally causes his ball to move in the following circumstances:

In measuring to determine which ball farther from hole—Rule 10-4

In searching for covered ball in hazard or for ball in casual water, ground under repair, etc.—Rule 12-1

In the process of repairing hole plug or ball mark—Rule 16-1c

In the process of removing loose impediment on putting green—Rule 18-2c

In the process of lifting ball under a Rule—Rule 20-1

In the process of placing or replacing ball under a Rule—Rule 20-3a

In complying with Rule 22 relating to lifting ball interfering with or assisting play

In removal of movable obstruction—Rule 24-1.

b. BALL MOVING AFTER ADDRESS

If a ball in play moves after the player has addressed it other than as a result of a stroke, he shall be deemed to have moved the ball and *shall incur a penalty stroke,* and the ball shall be played as it lies.

c. BALL MOVING AFTER LOOSE IMPEDIMENT TOUCHED

Through the green, if the ball moves after any loose impediment lying within a club-length of it has been touched by the player, his partner or either of their caddies and before the player has addressed it, the player shall be deemed to have moved the ball and *shall incur a penalty stroke.* The player shall replace the ball unless the movement of the ball occurs after he has begun his swing and he does not discontinue his swing.

On the putting green, if the ball moves in the process of removing any loose impediment, it shall be replaced without penalty.

a. DURING SEARCH

If, during search for a player's ball, it is moved by an opponent, his caddie or his <u>equipment</u>, no penalty is incurred and the player shall replace the ball.

b. OTHER THAN DURING SEARCH

If, other than during search for a ball, the ball is touched or moved by an opponent, his caddie or his <u>equipment</u>, except as otherwise provided in the Rules, *the opponent shall incur a penalty stroke.* The player shall replace the ball.

(Ball moved in measuring to determine which ball farther from the hole—Rule 10-4.)

(Playing a wrong ball—Rule 15-2.)

(Ball moved in complying with Rule 22 relating to lifting ball interfering with or assisting play.)

18-3

By Opponent, Caddie or Equipment in Match Play

If a competitor's ball is moved by a fellow-competitor, his caddie or his <u>equipment</u>, no penalty is incurred. The competitor shall replace his ball.

(Playing a wrong ball—Rule 15-3.)

18-4

By Fellow-Competitor, Caddie or Equipment in Stroke Play

If a player's ball at rest is moved by another ball, the player's ball shall be replaced.

PENALTY FOR BREACH OF RULE:
Match play—Loss of hole; Stroke play—Two strokes.

18-5

By Another Ball

* If a player who is required to replace a ball fails to do so, he shall incur the general penalty for breach of Rule 18 but no additional penalty under Rule 18 shall be applied.

Note: *If it is impossible to determine the spot on which a ball is to be placed, see Rule 20-3c.*

Two of the most consequential changes in the Rules adopted in 1984 occur in Rule 18. From now on, whenever a ball at rest is moved by another ball, it *must* be replaced. This applies to any form of play. Prior to 1984, the owner of the moved ball in single match play had the option of either replacing the ball or playing it from its new position. It may take some getting used to, but it's very simple: a ball at rest moved by another ball, anywhere on the course, in any variation of the game, *must* be replaced.

The second change eliminates an infamous trap in the Rules. Previously, when a player moved his ball in violation of the Rules (let's assume he accidentally kicked it during a search) and then failed to replace it, he picked up one penalty stroke for moving the ball and two more for failing to replace it. (He lost the hole in match play and still does.) Under the 1984 code, the maximum penalty in this situation in stroke play is two strokes—not three strokes.

Rule 18 takes us through the tangle of possibilities that occur when a ball at rest is moved. Let's consider each part of Rule 18:

18-1. By Outside Agency

When your ball is moved by a dog or by a golfer playing on another hole, it's been moved by an outside agency and you *must* replace the ball. No penalty. If you can't find your ball and think, but don't know for sure, that it may have been moved by an outside agency, all the available testimony and facts must be considered. To proceed under Rule 18-1, there must be "reasonable evidence" to that effect. In the absence of such evidence, the ball must be treated as a lost ball, which means stroke and distance.

18-2. By Player, Partner, Caddie or Equipment

Caution: If you so much as reach down and touch your ball except as the Rules allow, there is a penalty stroke. The onus is on you to know that the Rules have given you special license whenever you lift your ball. Notice that this Rule lists every instance (eight in all) when a player may move his ball accidentally and not be penalized. It's worth your while to know them.

Don't overlook the word "equipment." A Definition reveals that a golf cart is part of a player's equipment. When a player runs over his ball while driving a cart, he has violated this Rule.

The key word in clause b is "deemed." Once you've addressed the ball and it moves, that's it—a penalty. When it's windy or when the ball is perched in some precarious position, I take the precaution of not grounding my club and have therefore not addressed it. Remember —a Definition of "addressing the ball" tells us that grounding a club is part of addressing a ball through the green.

That word "deemed" pops up again in clause c. If you move a twig next to your ball and the ball then moves, you can argue yourself blue in the face in claiming that the movement of the twig didn't cause the ball to move. You are "deemed" to have caused the ball to move.

18-3. By Opponent, Caddie or Equipment in Match Play

If your opponent accidentally moves your ball while he's being good enough to help you look for it, he is not penalized. Fair enough. But if your opponent accidentally moves your ball in any other situation he incurs a penalty of one stroke. You must replace your ball in any case. If not, you lose the hole.

18-4. By Fellow-Competitor, Caddie or Equipment in Stroke Play

Now we're talking about stroke play, and the proper terminology calls for the use of "fellow-competitor," who is neither your "opponent" nor your "partner." He's someone you're paired with in stroke play; he becomes an outside agency in stroke play; and he's not penalized for moving your ball. Again, though, you must replace.

18-5. By Another Ball

This is the major 1984 change discussed above. Whenever a ball at rest is moved by another ball, the ball that was at rest has to be replaced.

RULE 19

BALL IN MOTION DEFLECTED OR STOPPED

An "outside agency" is any agency not part of the match or, in stroke play, not part of a competitor's side, and includes a referee, a marker, an observer or a forecaddie. Neither wind nor water is an outside agency.

"Equipment" is anything used, worn or carried by or for the player except any ball he has played and any small object, such as a coin or a tee, when used to mark the position of a ball or the extent of an area in which a ball is to be dropped. Equipment includes a golf cart, whether or not motorized. If such a cart is shared by more than one player, its status under the Rules is the same as that of a caddie employed by more than one player. See "Caddie."

19-1

By Outside Agency

If a ball in motion is accidentally deflected or stopped by any outside agency, it is a rub of the green, no penalty is incurred and the ball shall be played as it lies except:

a. If a ball in motion after a stroke other than on the putting green comes to rest in or on any moving or animate outside agency, the player shall, through the green or in a hazard, drop the ball, or on the putting green place the ball, as near as possible to the spot where the outside agency was when the ball came to rest in or on it, and

b. If a ball in motion after a stroke on the putting green is deflected or stopped by, or comes to rest in or on, any moving or animate outside agency, the stroke shall be canceled and the ball shall be replaced.

If the ball is not immediately recoverable, another ball may be substituted.

(Player's ball deflected or stopped by another ball at rest—see Rule 19-5.)

Note: *If the referee or the Committee determines that a ball has been deliberately deflected or stopped by an outside agency, including a fellow-competitor or his caddie, further procedure should be prescribed in equity under Rule 1-4.*

19-2

By Player, Partner, Caddie or Equipment

a. MATCH PLAY

If a player's ball is deflected or stopped by himself, his partner or either of their caddies or equipment, *he shall lose the hole.*

b. STROKE PLAY

If a competitor's ball is deflected or stopped by himself, his partner or either of their caddies or equipment, *the competitor shall incur a penalty of two strokes.* The ball shall be played as it lies, except when it comes to rest in or on the competitor's, his partner's or either of their caddies' clothes or equipment, in which case the competitor shall through the green or in a hazard drop the ball, or on the putting green place the ball, as near as possible to where the article was when the ball came to rest in or on it.

Exception: Dropped ball—see Rule 20-2a.

19-3
By Opponent, Caddie or Equipment in Match Play

a. PURPOSELY

If a player's ball is purposely deflected or stopped by an opponent, his caddie or his equipment, *the opponent shall lose the hole.*

Note: *In the case of a serious breach of Rule 19-3a, the Committee may impose a penalty of disqualification.*

b. ACCIDENTALLY

If a player's ball is accidentally deflected or stopped by an opponent, his caddie or his equipment, no penalty is incurred. The player may play the ball as it lies or, before another stroke is played by either side, cancel the stroke and replay the stroke (see Rule 20-5). If the ball has come to rest in or on the opponent's or his caddie's clothes or equipment, the player may through the green or in a hazard drop the ball, or on the putting green place the ball, as near as possible to where the article was when the ball came to rest in or on it.

Exception: Ball striking person attending flagstick—Rule 17-3b.

19-4
By Fellow-Competitor, Caddie or Equipment in Stroke Play

See Rule 19-1 regarding ball deflected by outside agency.

19-5
By a Ball at Rest

If a player's ball in motion is deflected or stopped by a ball at rest, the player shall play his ball as it lies. In stroke play, if both balls lay on the putting green prior to the stroke, *the player incurs a penalty of two strokes.* Otherwise, no penalty is incurred.

PENALTY FOR BREACH OF RULE:

Match play—Loss of hole; Stroke play—Two strokes.

Rule 18 just took us through the tangle of how to proceed when a ball *at rest* is moved. Rule 19 moves on to the problems that occur when a ball *in motion* is deflected or stopped.

19-1. By Outside Agency

The phrase "rub of the green" has drifted out of golf into everyday English, where it's generally taken to mean a bit of bad luck. Actually, it can work either way. If a ball bounces out of bounds after striking a cart path, that's one "rub of the green"; but if your ball is headed toward out of bounds and it's deflected by a tree onto the putting green, that too is a "rub of the green."

19-2. By Player, Partner, Caddie or Equipment

The standard match play penalty of loss of hole applies when a player's ball is deflected by himself, his partner, their caddies or their equipment (including a golf cart). In four-ball match play, only the player whose ball is involved is out of the hole.

In stroke play, it's a two-stroke penalty situation.

19-3. By Opponent, Caddie or Equipment in Match Play

Here we deal with a question of intent. If the deflection is deliberate, the opponent (or opposing team in four-ball play) loses the hole.

If the deflection is accidental, there is no penalty and the owner of the ball has an unusual choice. He can either play the ball as it lies or opt to cancel the stroke and play the stroke over.

19-4. By Fellow-Competitor, Caddie or Equipment in Stroke Play

It's just the same as in 19-1. There's no penalty *unless* the deflection is deliberate, in which case the offending party is in big trouble. A Committee, in equity, may disqualify a fellow-competitor who purposely stops another ball.

19-5. By a Ball at Rest

There's no penalty when a moving ball is deflected or stopped by a ball at rest, with one glaring exception: in stroke play only, when both balls are on the putting green before the stroke is played, the player whose ball is deflected suffers a two-stroke penalty. He plays his ball where it then lies; the other player must replace.

A couple of Rule 19 Decisions:

• A ball struck a piece of maintenance equipment and was deflected out of bounds. The player claimed she should not be penalized on the ground that the equipment wasn't supposed to be there.

Answer: The ball must be treated as out of bounds. A rather harsh rub of the green, but there you have it.

• Jack Sargent of Atlanta, an authority on the Rules, has asked many questions that resulted in Decisions. Here's one:

A player, in stroke play, hits a ball off line; the ball first hits his bag and then his caddie. Is the player penalized four strokes for two violations of Rule 19-2?

Answer: No. Generally, a single penalty is applied to several instances of a breach of a Rule in connection with a single stroke. For example, soling the club by touching the ground or water with it time and again in a hazard entails a single penalty. Ah, but in this case, if the ball had struck his caddie and then gone out of bounds, he would have violated two different Rules and paid the consequences for both.

RELIEF SITUATIONS AND PROCEDURE

LIFTING, DROPPING AND PLACING; PLAYING FROM WRONG PLACE

20-1

Lifting

A ball to be lifted under the Rules may be lifted by the player, his partner or another person authorized by the player. In any such case, the player shall be responsible for any breach of the Rules.

The position of the ball shall be marked before it is lifted under a Rule which requires it to be replaced. If it is not marked, the player *shall incur a penalty of one stroke* and the ball shall be replaced. If it is not replaced, *the player shall incur the general penalty* for breach of this Rule but no additional penalty under Rule 20-1 shall be applied.

If a ball is accidentally moved in the process of lifting it under a Rule, no penalty shall be incurred and the ball shall be replaced.

Note: *The position of a lifted ball should be marked, if feasible, by placing a ball-marker or other small object immediately behind the ball. If the ball-marker interferes with the play, <u>stance</u> or <u>stroke</u> of another player, it should be placed one or more clubhead-lengths to one side.*

20-2

Dropping and Re-dropping

a. By Whom and How

A ball to be dropped under the Rules shall be dropped by the player himself. He shall stand erect, hold the ball at shoulder height and arm's length and drop it. If a ball is dropped by any other person or in any other manner and the error is not corrected as provided in Rule 20-6, *the player shall incur a penalty stroke.*

If the ball touches the player, his partner, either of their caddies or their equipment before or after it strikes the ground, the ball shall be re-dropped, without penalty.

(Taking action to influence position or movement of ball— Rule 1-2.)

How to Drop

*Here's the new dropping procedure, introduced in 1984. Simply extend your arm horizontally and drop the ball. That's all there is to it. You can do it off to one side (*left) *or directly in front of you (*right). *But do remember* not *to use the pre-1984 procedure of dropping over your shoulder.*

91

b. WHERE TO DROP

When a ball is to be dropped, it shall be dropped as near as possible to the spot where the ball lay, but not nearer the hole, except when a Rule permits it to be dropped elsewhere. If a ball is to be dropped in a hazard, the ball shall be dropped in and come to rest in that hazard.

c. WHEN TO RE-DROP

A dropped ball shall be re-dropped without penalty if it:

(i) rolls into a hazard;

(ii) rolls out of a hazard;

(iii) rolls onto a putting green;

(iv) rolls out of bounds;

(v) rolls back into the condition from which relief was taken under Rule 24-2 (immovable obstruction) or Rule 25 (abnormal ground conditions and wrong putting green);

(vi) rolls and comes to rest more than two club-lengths from where it first struck the ground; or

(vii) rolls and comes to rest nearer the hole than is permitted by the Rules.

If the ball again rolls into such position, it shall be placed as near as possible to the spot where it first struck the ground when re-dropped.

20-3
Placing and Replacing

a. BY WHOM AND WHERE

A ball to be placed under the Rules shall be placed by the player or his partner. A ball to be replaced shall be replaced by the player, his partner or the person who lifted or moved it on the spot where the ball lay. In any such case, the player shall be responsible for any breach of the Rules.

If a ball is accidentally moved in the process of placing or replacing it under a Rule, no penalty shall be incurred and the ball shall be replaced.

b. LIE OF BALL TO BE PLACED OR REPLACED ALTERED

Except in a bunker, if the original lie of a ball to be placed or replaced has been altered, the ball shall be placed in the nearest lie most similar to that which it originally occupied, not more than one club-length from the original lie and not nearer the hole. In a bunker, the original lie shall be re-created as nearly as possible and the ball shall be placed in that lie.

c. SPOT NOT DETERMINABLE

If it is impossible to determine the spot where the ball is to be placed, the ball shall through the green or in a hazard be dropped, or on the putting green be placed, as near as possible to the place where it lay but not nearer the hole.

d. BALL FAILS TO REMAIN ON SPOT

If a ball when placed fails to remain on the spot on which it was placed, it shall be replaced without penalty. If it still fails to remain on that spot, it shall be placed at the nearest spot not nearer the hole where it can be placed at rest.

PENALTY FOR BREACH OF RULE 20-1, -2 OR -3:

Match play—Loss of hole; Stroke play—Two strokes.

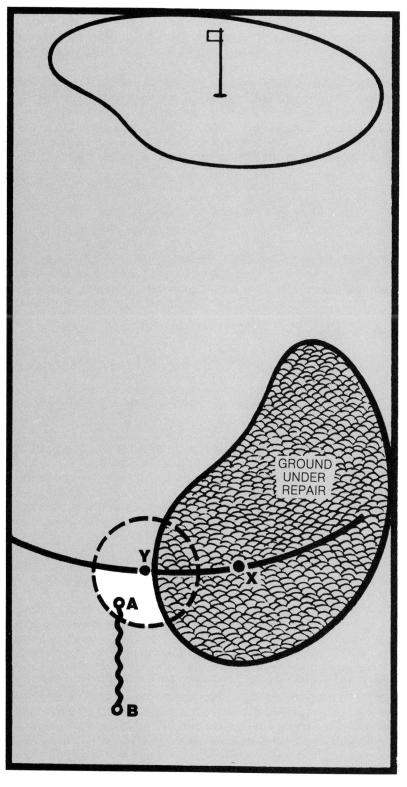

Geometry of Ball Dropping

Here's a common drop situation. The ball lies in ground under repair at X. First the player determines the nearest point of relief, which in this illustration is at Y— just outside the ground under repair area. The player must drop within one club-length of Y, but he can't drop in the shaded area because all of that area is either closer to the hole or within ground under repair. That leaves him with the white area. The ball remains in play if it's dropped at Point A even though it rolls outside the circle to Point B— which is less than two club-lengths from A.
(R. 25-1b)

GROUND UNDER REPAIR

20-4
Ball in Play When Dropped or Placed

A ball dropped or placed under a Rule governing the particular case is in play.

20-5
Playing Next Stroke from Where Previous Stroke Played

When, under the Rules, a player elects or is required to play his next stroke from where a previous stroke was played, he shall proceed as follows: If the stroke is to be played from the teeing ground, the ball to be played shall be played from anywhere within the teeing ground and may be teed; if the stroke is to be played from through the green or a hazard, it shall be dropped; if the stroke is to be played on the putting green, it shall be placed.

PENALTY FOR BREACH OF RULE 20-5:
Match play—Loss of hole; Stroke play—Two strokes.

20-6
Lifting Ball Wrongly Dropped or Placed

A ball dropped or placed in a wrong place or otherwise not in accordance with the Rules but not played may be lifted, without penalty, and the player shall then proceed correctly.

In match play, if, before the opponent plays his next stroke, the player fails to inform him that the ball has been lifted, *the player shall lose the hole.*

20-7
Playing from Wrong Place

For a ball played outside teeing ground, see Rule 11-3.

a. MATCH PLAY

If a player plays a stroke with a ball which has been dropped or placed under an applicable Rule but in a wrong place, *he shall lose the hole.*

b. STROKE PLAY

If a competitor plays a stroke with a ball which has been (i) dropped or placed under an applicable Rule but in a wrong place or (ii) moved and not replaced in a case where the Rules require replacement, *he shall incur the penalty prescribed by the relevant Rule* and play out the hole with the ball. If a serious breach of the relevant Rule is involved, *the competitor shall be disqualified,* unless the breach has been rectified as provided in the next paragraph.

If a serious breach may be involved and the competitor has not made a stroke on the next teeing ground or, in the case of the last hole of the round, has not left the putting green, the competitor may rectify any such serious breach by *adding two penalty strokes to his score,* dropping or playing a second ball in accordance with the Rules and playing out the hole. The competitor should play out the hole with both balls. On completion of the round the competitor shall report the facts immediately to the Committee; if he fails to do so, *he shall be disqualified.* The Committee shall determine whether a serious breach of the Rule was involved and, accordingly, whether the score with the second ball shall count.

Note: *Penalty strokes incurred by playing the ball ruled not to count and strokes subsequently taken with that ball shall be disregarded.*

20-1. Lifting

Rule 20, to be used properly, requires a good deal of prior knowledge. First, the ball should not be lifted unless the golfer knows full well that the Rules authorize him to pick it up. Second, having lifted the ball, he should know whether the ball should be dropped or placed when it is put back into play. (If it is to be replaced, he must mark its position.) If the former, he should know where he may drop it. In some cases the ball must be dropped as near as possible to the spot from which it was lifted, such as when the ball is embedded in a fairway; in others there's a one-club-length tolerance from the nearest point of relief, as when taking relief from ground under repair; and in others there's a two-club-length leeway—e.g., dropping on either side of a lateral water hazard. It's useful to remember that when the extent of relief is one club-length, there is no penalty; when the extent is two club-lengths, a penalty is involved.

20-2. Dropping and Re-dropping

Three cheers for the new dropping rule. Gone forever are the silly and tricky arguments about what constitutes facing the hole and about the requirements of the old "over the shoulder" procedure.

The new dropping method is almost blinding in its simplicity and common sense. The player only has to stand erect, hold the ball at shoulder height and arm's length—and drop it. It doesn't matter what he's facing or where he's looking.

But be wary of getting caught up in a lifetime of habit. If you drop the ball in the old manner you will incur a penalty stroke—unless you remember, or are reminded, to pick it up and drop correctly, a corrective action permitted by Clause 6 of this Rule.

It often happens that when a player drops a ball, the slope of the ground is such that the ball rolls more than two club-lengths or nearer the hole. Rule 20-2c calls for a three-step procedure:

1. Ball is dropped and it rolls nearer the hole or more than two club-lengths.

2. Ball is dropped again and it again rolls nearer the hole or more than two club-lengths.

3. Ball is then *placed* on the spot where it first touched the ground when it was dropped the second time.

Rule 20-2c pulls together all the mandatory "re-drops."

20-3. Placing and Replacing

Placing isn't as complicated as dropping, but it can lead to problems. Rule 20-3b deals with what to do when the lie of a ball to be placed has been "altered." Imagine that your ball and your opponent's touch each other in a fairway. He's away, so you mark and lift your ball. When he plays, he takes a divot and effectively demolishes your lie. You don't have to place the ball in the hole, nor do you replace the divot and put your ball on it. What you do is place your ball as near as possible to its original position in "the nearest lie most similar to that which it originally occupied, not more than one club-length from the original lie and not nearer the hole."

In a bunker, however, the procedure is dramatically different. When a lie is "altered"—which happens inevitably when balls come to rest adjacent to each other—the original lie is to be *re-created* as nearly

Marking a Ball

When a ball anywhere on the course is to be lifted, its position must be marked if the ball is to be replaced. I use a coin (1) and place it immediately behind the ball (2) before lifting the ball (3). When the coin interferes with another player, it's moved the length of one or more putterheads. To make sure I can replace the coin exactly where it was, I first select a reference point—often a tree (4)—before setting down my putter between the coin and the reference point (5). The last step is to move the coin (6). (R. 20-1)

as possible. This means that the player gets to smooth the sand and place his ball atop it, if that's the way it was originally; conversely, it means he has to plug his ball into the sand if that was its original lie.

20-4. Ball in Play When Dropped or Placed

Jack Nicklaus is superb when it comes to understanding and applying the Rules, but he once cost himself dearly by failing to understand Rule 20-4. Worse yet, it happened in the Masters on the 15th hole. His ball had come to rest against a spectator's stool, and the ball moved when the stool was moved. Jack then correctly replaced his ball on a bank that sloped sharply toward the green. (See Rule 24-1.) There was very little grass to support the ball and Jack was faced with a delicate little pitch. It was not likely he'd get down in two. Ben Crenshaw, with whom Jack was paired, was away, and as Ben prepared to play and then did play, Jack surveyed the green. When he looked back, he saw that his ball had rolled down the slope about fifteen yards to the edge of the green. The ball had actually been at rest for about one minute.

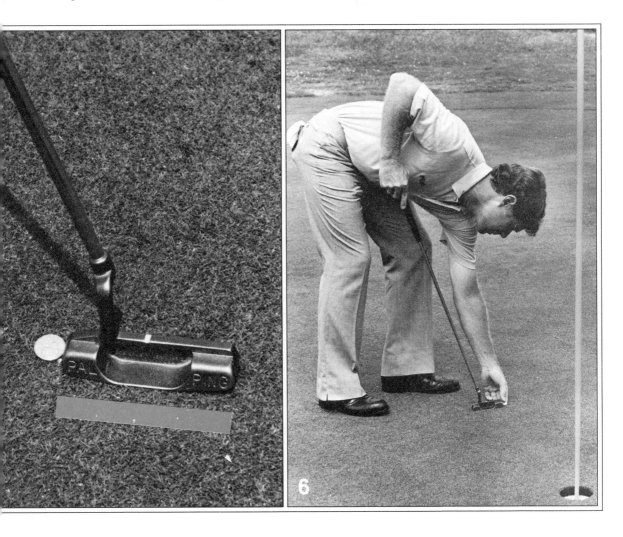

6

Jack's instinctive sportsmanship suggested to him that he had to put the ball back up on the slope. He conferred with an official, and they agreed that the ball had to be replaced. They were wrong! Once the ball was properly placed and remained at rest for a few seconds, it was in play. When it subsequently moved, it was in play at the new position and should have been played from there. As it happened, Jack took three to get down from the slope and made a par 5. Had he played from the edge of the green, he would have been putting for an eagle 3 and almost surely would have made a birdie 4. Moreover, Jack's sportsmanship could have caused him two penalty strokes, under Rule 18, for picking up his ball when he was not entitled to, and for failing to replace it on the spot from which it was lifted. There was no penalty, since a player is entitled to assume that an official's ruling is correct.

Rule 20-6. Lifting Ball Wrongly Dropped or Placed

Rule 20-6 gets the player off the hook if he errs in dropping or placing, provided he hasn't made the next stroke. Thus if a player taking relief from a cart path—an obstruction—drops more than one club-length away from the nearest point of relief and immediately learns of the error, he can correct the mistake without penalty.

Rule 20-7. Playing from Wrong Place

The wording of Rule 20-7 is a little on the heavy side. An example of a "wrong place" incident is when a ball is dropped more than one club-length from the nearest point of relief from interference by a cart path.

When that happens in match play, the penalty is loss of hole as soon as the offender plays a stroke.

But in stroke play the penalty is two strokes, because that's what is called for by the Rule governing obstructions. If, after making the next stroke, the "wrong place" violation is made known to the player, he must play on and hole out. He can't rectify the mistake once the stroke is made, unless a "serious breach" is involved.

A "serious breach" is one that would give a player an inordinate advantage. Imagine a water hazard thirty yards in diameter right up against the green. The ball enters the hazard in such a way that the player, in taking relief, must drop behind the hazard. But let's assume the player instead drops on the far side of the hazard, next to the green. He hasn't negotiated the hazard. That's a serious breach, and unless it's rectified as permitted in Rule 20-7, the penalty in stroke play is disqualification.

RULE 21

CLEANING BALL

A ball may be cleaned when lifted as follows:
Upon suspension of play in accordance with Rule 6-8b;
For identification under Rule 12-2, but the ball may be cleaned only to the extent necessary for identification;

On the <u>putting green</u> under Rule 16-1b;
For relief from an <u>obstruction</u> under Rule 24-1b or -2b;
For relief from abnormal ground conditions or wrong putting green under Rules 25-1b, -2 and -3;
For relief from a <u>water hazard</u> under Rule 26;
For relief for an unplayable ball under Rule 28; or
Under a Local Rule permitting cleaning the ball.

If the player cleans his ball during the play of a hole except as permitted under this Rule, *he shall incur a penalty of one stroke* and the ball, if lifted, shall be replaced.

If a player who is required to replace a ball fails to do so, *he shall incur the penalty* for breach of Rule 20-3a, but no additional penalty under Rule 21 shall be applied.

This Rule isolates the eight situations which permit a player to clean his ball after lifting it.

Notice that the penalty, in both stroke and match play, for an unauthorized cleansing, is only one stroke.

You want a couple of examples of when it's wrong to clean a ball after it's lifted? You can't clean when you lift your ball from an "apron" or, for that matter, from anywhere other than the putting green because it interferes with the line of play or stroke of another player. Another: you can't clean your ball—again off the putting green—before you replace it after it's been moved by another ball.

RULE 22

BALL INTERFERING WITH OR ASSISTING PLAY

Any player may:
a. Lift his ball if he considers that it might assist any other player or
b. Have any other ball lifted if he considers that it might interfere with his play or assist the play of any other player, but this may not be done while another ball is in motion. In stroke play, a player required to lift his ball may play first rather than lift. A ball lifted under this Rule shall be replaced.

If a ball is accidentally moved in complying with this Rule, no penalty is incurred and the ball shall be replaced.

PENALTY FOR BREACH OF RULE:
Match play—Loss of hole; Stroke play—Two strokes.

As far as I'm concerned, the most significant change in the 1984 Rules is contained in Rule 22. It consolidates all the situations that concern a ball interfering with or assisting play.

Better than that, it introduces uniformity into the various forms of play. From now on, an opponent or fellow-competitor is always permitted to lift his ball if he considers that it might assist any other player.

Thus is wiped from the book the old maxim that in singles match play the player who is away "controls" the opponent's ball in the sense of having the right to require him to leave it or lift it. No longer can the ball adjacent to or beyond a hole be used as a kind of backstop. The owner of the potential backstop can protect himself by lifting his ball. But if he doesn't and the ball is moved by the putted ball of an opponent, the moved ball *must* be replaced. The owner of the moved ball does not have the option of playing it from its new place.

In four-ball play, be it match or stroke, that principle applies just as it did prior to 1984. Any player can have any ball lifted if he thinks it might interfere with his play or, because of its location, help the play of an opponent.

RULE 23

LOOSE IMPEDIMENTS

Definition

"Loose impediments" are natural objects such as stones, leaves, twigs, branches and the like, dung, worms and insects and casts or heaps made by them, provided they are not fixed or growing, are not solidly embedded and do not adhere to the ball.

Sand and loose soil are loose impediments on the putting green but not elsewhere.

Snow and ice are either casual water or loose impediments, at the option of the player.

Dew is not a loose impediment.

23-1

Relief

Except when both the loose impediment and the ball lie in or touch a hazard, any loose impediment may be removed without penalty. If the ball moves, see Rule 18-2c.

When a player's ball is in motion, a loose impediment on his line of play shall not be removed.

PENALTY FOR BREACH OF RULE:

Match play—Loss of hole; Stroke play—Two strokes.

(Searching for ball in hazard—Rule 12-1.)

(Touching line of putt—Rule 16-1a.)

Rule 23 is easy to understand and use so long as you know that loose impediments, according to the Definition, are natural objects not fixed or growing, not solidly embedded and not adhering to the ball. That's why the relevant Definitions are repeated prior to the actual Rules in the 1984 code. There they are instantly accessible.

The prohibition against moving loose impediments in hazards is purposely severe. Generally speaking, when you've hit your ball into a hazard, you've made a mistake and you have to deal with the problem directly. That means not removing leaves or stones that happen to interfere with your stroke.

There was a funny incident at the 1977 U.S. Open when Ben Crenshaw's ball came to rest in a kind of nest of ice cubes dumped out of a cup by a spectator. The Definition says snow and ice can be treated

A Bad Break
Because it's in a hazard this twig may not be moved. The same applies to leaves, stones and other loose impediments—all natural objects. In a hazard you can't so much as touch one with your club on your backswing. Of course if the twig were magically changed into a cigar, it could be removed because a cigar is an obstruction—an artificial object. (R. 13-4)

as either loose impediments or casual water, which calls for a different and more generous relief procedure. The USGA officials debated whether "ice" referred only to wintertime ice. But since this happened in Tulsa during mid-June, the debate soon became moot as the cubes were transformed into casual water.

RULE 24

OBSTRUCTIONS

An "obstruction" is anything artificial, including the artificial surfaces and sides of roads and paths, except: **Definition**

    a. Objects defining <u>out of bounds</u>, such as walls, fences, stakes and railings;

    b. Any part of an immovable artificial object which is out of bounds; and

    c. Any construction declared by the Committee to be an integral part of the course.

A player may obtain relief from a movable <u>obstruction</u> as follows:

24-1

Movable Obstruction

    a. If the ball does not lie in or on the obstruction, the obstruction may be removed; if the ball moves, no penalty is incurred and the ball shall be replaced.

101

Movable Obstruction

A bench is artificial and therefore an obstruction. Obviously I want relief. Since this bench can readily be moved, it's a movable obstruction. Since it's movable, I do not have the option of dropping away from the bench without penalty. If the ball was up against a leg and happened to move when I set the bench aside, I would replace it without penalty. (R. 24-1)

b. If the ball lies in or on the obstruction, the ball may be lifted, without penalty, and the obstruction removed. The ball shall <u>through the green</u> or in a <u>hazard</u> be dropped, or on the <u>putting green</u> be placed, as near as possible to the spot directly under the place where the ball lay in or on the obstruction, but not nearer the hole.

The ball may be cleaned when lifted for relief under Rule 24-1b.

When a ball is in motion, an obstruction on the player's line of play other than an attended flagstick and equipment of the players shall not be removed.

a. INTERFERENCE

Interference by an immovable <u>obstruction</u> occurs when a ball lies in or on the obstruction, or so close to the obstruction that the obstruction interferes with the player's <u>stance</u> or the area of his intended swing. If the player's ball lies on the <u>putting green</u>, interference also occurs if an immovable obstruction on the putting green intervenes on his line of putt. Otherwise, intervention on the line of play is not, of itself, interference under this Rule.

b. RELIEF

Except when the ball lies in or touches a <u>water hazard</u> or a <u>lateral water hazard</u>, a player may obtain relief from interference by an immovable <u>obstruction</u>, without penalty, as follows:

(i) *Through the Green:* If the ball lies <u>through the green</u>, the point on the <u>course</u> nearest to where the ball lies shall be determined (without crossing over, through or under the obstruction) which (a) is not nearer the hole, (b) avoids interference (as defined) and (c) is not in a <u>hazard</u> or on a <u>putting green</u>. The player shall lift the ball and drop it within one club-length of the point thus determined on ground which fulfills (a), (b) and (c) above.

Note: *The prohibition against crossing over, through or under the <u>obstruction</u> does not apply to the artificial surfaces and sides of roads and paths or when the ball lies in or on the obstruction.*

(ii) *In a Bunker:* If the ball lies in or touches a <u>bunker</u>, the player shall lift and drop the ball in accordance with Clause (i) above, except that the ball must be dropped in the bunker.

(iii) *On the Putting Green:* If the ball lies on the <u>putting green</u>, the player shall lift the ball and place it in the nearest position to where it lay which affords relief from interference, but not nearer the hole nor in a hazard.

The ball may be cleaned when lifted for relief under Rule 24-2b.

(Ball rolling back into condition from which relief taken—see Rule 20-2c(v).)

Exception: A player may not obtain relief under Rule 24-2b if (a) it is clearly unreasonable for him to play a stroke be-

24-2

Immovable Obstruction

cause of interference by anything other than an immovable obstruction or (b) interference by an immovable obstruction would occur only through use of an unnecessarily abnormal stance, swing or direction of play.

Note: *If a ball lies in or touches a <u>water hazard</u> (including a <u>lateral water hazard</u>), the player is not entitled to relief without penalty from interference by an immovable obstruction. The player shall play the ball as it lies or proceed under Rule 26-1.*

PENALTY FOR BREACH OF RULE:
Match play—Loss of hole; Stroke play—Two strokes.

Golfers tend to pounce on the word "relief" with a sense of reckless joy, ignoring the harsh reality that the relief is limited and precise, and is not a carte blanche solution to any and every inconvenience caused by artificial objects (obstructions).

First, there are the limitations contained in the Definition, which states that three kinds of artificial objects are *not* obstructions. Therefore, no relief is provided when there is interference by

a. any object used to define out of bounds, including movable objects such as white stakes;

b. any part of an immovable object which is out of bounds;

c. any construction declared by the Committee to be an integral part of the course. The onus is on the Committee to make any such limitation clear on a score card or wherever Local Rules are posted.

I'm entitled to relief without penalty in (1) because the stone wall interferes with my stance. The same applies in (2) because now there's interference with my swing. But I get no relief in (3) because the obstruction, although it's on my line, does not interfere with my stance or swing. When you take relief from an immovable obstruction (4), you establish the nearest point, no nearer the hole, where there is no interference, and drop within one club-length of that point.

Another important limitation in Rule 24 denies relief when an immovable obstruction is on the line of play but is not close enough to interfere with the stance or swing. I'm afraid golfers are misled by what they see on television when "line of sight" relief (dropping to the side of an obstruction on your line) is granted by Local Rule from what are called "temporary immovable obstructions." These include pro-tour necessities such as scoreboards, grandstands and television towers, which are necessarily installed very close to playing areas. There is no such thing as "line of sight" relief in everyday play through the green.

A third limitation has to do with the maximum relief that is available when a ball lies in or on an obstruction, or so close that it interferes with the stance or swing. Rule 24 offers a procedure for finding "the point on the course nearest to where the ball lies" and then allows a drop within one club-length of that point. Neither the point nor the spot at which the ball is dropped can be nearer the hole than the ball's original resting place, in a hazard or on a putting green, yet both must be far enough away so as to avoid the very interference for which the relief is granted. See the illustrations and captions accompanying Rule 24 for an exposition of how to drop away from obstructions.

A fourth limitation—and one that is new in 1984—denies relief from immovable obstructions when a ball is in a water hazard or lateral water hazard. This eliminates what used to be an enormously complicated section of a Definition concerning bridges and "artificially surfaced banks." It's easy now: If your ball is within a water hazard, and there's interference by an immovable obstruction, either play it as it lies or drop out of the hazard, with a one-stroke penalty, under Rule 26.

Some other guidelines and cautions in applying Rule 24:

● Whenever the artificial object—for instance a bench—is movable, it may be removed. A player does not have the option of lifting and dropping the ball away from a movable obstruction. That might be to his advantage if the ball lies poorly.

On the other hand, the relief from movable obstructions is generous in that those on the line of play may be removed. Common movable obstructions on the pro tour include gallery stakes, ropes, TV and telephone wires, and various signs.

● Relief from movable obstructions (bottles, cigarette butts, etc.) in hazards is simple. You simply remove them.

● One of the most common obstruction situations arises when the stance or swing is interfered with by wires or ropes supporting young trees. Understand that the relief applies to the wires or rope but not to the tree itself, which means that (a) the "nearest point" must be related to the interfering artificial object and not to the tree, and (b) if the wire or rope doesn't interfere, there is no relief.

Obstructions in Hazards
It's okay to remove obstructions—artificial things—from hazards. Obvious examples include rakes, paper cups and cigarette stubs. If the ball moves in the process you must replace it, but without penalty.

Sprinkler Heads

Since my stance is on a sprinkler head (1), I can take relief without penalty. I've established the nearest point (2) and marked it with a tee. The extent of relief, one club-length, is marked (3) with a second tee. There's another illustration (4) of the new dropping procedure—within the area marked by the tees. When a sprinkler head off a putting green is on your line but does not interfere with your stance or swing (5), there is no free relief. Go ahead and chip the ball. (R. 24-2)

• Watch out for sprinkler heads and the plastic caps of irrigation systems located on the aprons of putting greens. The impulse, almost irresistible, is to lift and place the ball off to the side when one of these caps is on your line, especially when your ball is also on the apron and you want to putt it. Fact is, there is no relief. Read it and weep.

Some handy Rule 24 Decisions:

• The player's ball is nestled in a coiled hose—a movable obstruction—but he erroneously treats it as an immovable obstruction and drops away instead of moving the hose.

Answer: The player lifted a ball when he was not entitled to. Under Rule 18-2 he incurs a penalty stroke and has to replace the ball. The player should have moved the hose.

• A player's ball was four or five inches away from a flat sprinkler head that did not interfere with his stance or swing. The player claimed relief, however, on the ground that the covering constituted a mental hazard.

Answer: He doesn't get it. Mental interference by an obstruction does not entitle the player to relief.

• Is it permissible to drop from an obstruction in the rough into a fairway, if that's where a correct drop might lead you?

Answer: Yes. There is no distinction in the Rules between fairway and rough; both are covered by the term "through the green."

● A player asked for relief from a bird's nest.

Answer: The USGA, in a burst of tenderness, tersely said that the nest can be treated as an immovable obstruction (whether or not the nest is occupied)—happily ignoring the reality that a nest is anything but artificial.

● Irrigation control boxes are often built near the edges of fairways. Is it proper to adopt a Local Rule granting "line of flight" relief?

Answer: No, since the boxes are permanent and therefore not analogous to such things as tents and television equipment, which are given special treatment.

● Jack Crist of Charlotte, North Carolina, when Chairman of the USGA Rules of Golf Committee, thought that the term "the point on the course nearest to where the ball lies" needed clarification, when it first appeared in the Rules, and many agreed.

A Decision was published: "When the position of a ball is such that there is interference by an immovable obstruction, there is a specific point on the course (not nearer the hole, nor on the putting green nor in a hazard) nearest to which the ball originally lay at which, if the ball were so positioned, interference would cease to exist. The point is 'the point on the course nearest to where the ball lies.'

Relief from Cart Paths

An artificially surfaced cart path is an immovable obstruction. I'm entitled to relief even if the ball is off the path, but I have to stand on it. (1). Here's how to take relief from the situation shown in (2): I establish the nearest point by sticking in a tee at that point, measure one club-length and mark the width of the area in which I can drop by inserting another tee (3). Then I drop (4) between and behind the tees. There's only one *nearest point of relief*. In illustration (5) the nearest point is where I'm standing, not where my friend is standing, because the ball is closer to the point on the left. (But if it was closer to the right, you'd have to go to the right—if you want relief—even though the tree poses a problem.) But let's turn it around, imagine that both of us are left-handed players, and the ball is in the same place (6). Now the nearest point shifts over to the right. A key, of course, is that the stance must be taken off the path.

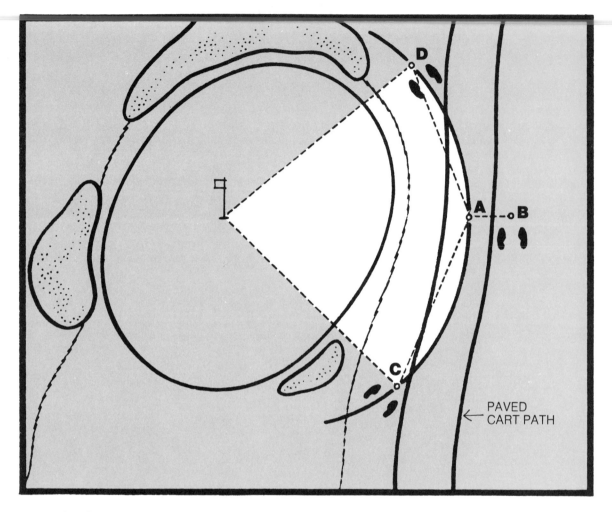

Dropping from an Obstruction

Three spots might qualify as the nearest point of relief when there's interference by an immovable obstruction, such as a paved cart path. The point that is the shortest distance from the ball (A) must be used. The three possibilities are behind the obstruction (B); on an arc to the left (C); and on an arc to the right (D). Since line A–B is shorter than lines A–C and A–D, the nearest point of relief is B. The same principle applies when relief is taken from ground under repair and casual water. (R. 24-2b)

"If the ball does not lie in or on an obstruction and an artificially surfaced road or path is not involved, the point in question is the nearest one avoiding interference which can be reached without crossing over, through or under the obstruction.

"In determining the nearest point where interference would cease to exist, the club with which the player would expect to play the next stroke must be used. In measuring the one club-length from the nearest point, the player may use any club selected for the round.

"The prohibition against crossing over, through or under an obstruction does not apply when measuring from the nearest point the one club-length within which the player must drop the ball."

RULE 25

ABNORMAL GROUND CONDITIONS AND WRONG PUTTING GREEN

Definitions

"Casual water" is any temporary accumulation of water on the course which is visible before or after the player takes his stance and is not in a water hazard. Snow and ice are either casual water or loose impediments, at the option of the player. Dew is not casual water.

"Ground under repair" is any portion of the course so marked by order of the Committee or so declared by its authorized representative. It includes material piled for removal and a hole made by a greenkeeper, even if not so marked. Stakes and lines defining ground under repair are in such ground.

Note 1: *Grass cuttings and other material left on the course which have been abandoned and are not intended to be removed are not ground under repair unless so marked.*

Note 2: *The Committee may make a Local Rule prohibiting play from ground under repair.*

25-1

Casual Water, Ground Under Repair and Certain Damage to Course

a. INTERFERENCE
Interference by casual water, ground under repair or a hole, cast or runway made by a burrowing animal, a reptile or a bird occurs when a ball lies in or touches any of these conditions or when the condition interferes with the player's stance or the area of his intended swing.

If the player's ball lies on the putting green, interference also occurs if such condition on the putting green intervenes on his line of putt.

If interference exists, the player may either play the ball as it lies (unless prohibited by Local Rule) or take relief as provided in Clause b.

b. RELIEF
If the player elects to take relief, he shall proceed as follows:

113

Casual Water
*The ball lies in casual water
(1), so I'm entitled to take
relief by first determining the
nearest point that both avoids
the casual water and is not
nearer the hole. I haven't
reached that point in (2)
because my foot is in the
water. That's interference. But
in (3) I've determined the
point and have marked it with
a tee. I measure one club-
length from that point in (4),
lift the club, and—before
dropping—I clean the ball
(5).*

114

(i) *Through the Green:* If the ball lies through the green, the point on the course nearest to where the ball lies shall be determined which (a) is not nearer the hole, (b) avoids interference by the condition, and (c) is not in a hazard or on a putting green. The player shall lift the ball and drop it without penalty within one club-length of the point thus determined on ground which fulfills (a), (b) and (c) above.

(ii) *In a Hazard:* If the ball lies in or touches a hazard, the player shall lift and drop the ball either:

(a) Without penalty, in the hazard, as near as possible to the spot where the ball lay, but not nearer the hole, on ground which affords maximum available relief from the condition;

or

(b) *Under penalty of one stroke,* outside the hazard, keeping the spot where the ball lay directly between himself and the hole.

Exception: If a ball lies in or touches a water hazard (in-

cluding a <u>lateral water hazard</u>), the player is not entitled to relief without penalty from a hole, cast or runway made by a burrowing animal, reptile or a bird. The player shall play the ball as it lies or proceed under Rule 26-1.

(iii) *On the Putting Green:* If the ball lies on the <u>putting green</u>, the player shall lift the ball and place it without penalty in the nearest position to where it lay which affords maximum available relief from the condition, but not nearer the hole nor in a <u>hazard</u>.

The ball may be cleaned when lifted under Rule 25-1b.

(Ball rolling back into condition from which relief taken—see Rule 20-2c(v).)

Exception: A player may not obtain relief under Rule 25-1b if (a) it is clearly unreasonable for him to play a stroke because of interference by anything other than a condition covered by Rule 25-1a or (b) interference by such a condition would occur only through use of an unnecessarily abnormal stance, swing or direction of play.

c. Ball Lost Under Condition Covered by Rule 25-1

It is a question of fact whether a ball lost after having been struck toward a condition covered by Rule 25-1 is lost under such condition. In order to treat the ball as lost under such condition, there must be reasonable evidence to that effect. In the absence of such evidence, the ball must be treated as a lost ball and Rule 27 applies.

(i) *Outside a Hazard*—If a ball is lost outside a <u>hazard</u> under a condition covered by Rule 25-1, the player may take relief as follows: the point on the <u>course</u> nearest to where the ball last crossed the margin of the area shall be determined which (a) is not nearer the hole than where the ball last crossed the margin, (b) avoids interference by the condition and (c) is not in a hazard or on a <u>putting green</u>. He shall drop a ball without penalty within one club-length of the point thus determined on ground which fulfills (a), (b) and (c) above.

(ii) *In a Hazard*—If a ball is lost in a <u>hazard</u> under a condition covered by Rule 25-1, the player may drop a ball either:

(a) Without penalty, in the hazard, as near as possible to the point at which the ball last crossed the margin of the area, but not nearer the hole, on ground which affords maximum available relief from the condition

or

(b) *Under penalty of one stroke,* outside the hazard, keeping the spot at which the ball last crossed the margin of the hazard directly between himself and the hole.

Exception: If a ball lies in a <u>water hazard</u> (including a <u>lateral water hazard</u>), the player is not entitled to relief without penalty for a ball lost in a hole, cast or runway made by a burrowing animal, a reptile or a bird. The player shall proceed under Rule 26-1.

A ball embedded in its own pitch-mark in any closely mown area <u>through the green</u> may be lifted, cleaned and dropped, without penalty, as near as possible to the spot where it lay but not nearer the hole. "Closely mown area" means any area of the <u>course,</u> including paths through the rough, cut to fairway height or less.

25-2
Embedded Ball

If a ball lies on a <u>putting green</u> other than that of the hole being played, the point on the <u>course</u> nearest to where the ball lies shall be determined which (a) is not nearer the hole and (b) is not in a <u>hazard</u> or on a putting green. The player shall lift the ball and drop it without penalty within one club-

25-3
Wrong Putting Green

Ground Under Repair
The relief procedure for ground under repair and casual water are the same. I can take relief if the ball is in ground under repair or if I have to stand in the area. Relief, of course, is optional. If I like the lie, I'll simply play the ball without taking relief. (R. 25-1)

117

length of the point thus determined on ground which fulfills (a) and (b) above. The ball may be cleaned when so lifted.

Note: *Unless otherwise prescribed by the Committee, the term "a putting green other than that of the hole being played" includes a practice putting green or pitching green on the course.*

PENALTY FOR BREACH OF RULE:
Match play—Loss of hole; Stroke play—Two strokes.

Rule 25 now logically consolidates in one section three kinds of relief procedures that previously were sprinkled in three different Rules.

There is one substantive change in these procedures. That concerns relief from burrowing animals' holes for a ball lying in a water hazard. Relief without penalty is no longer granted, and I applaud that heartily. It used to gall me to see a player whose ball was barely playable in a water hazard take his stance on a tiny little ground-squirrel hole, claim relief, and then drop in a much more favorable position.

25-1. Casual Water, Ground Under Repair and Certain Damage to the Course

The word "interference" doesn't always click as it should with readers of the Rules of Golf. "Gets in the way of" or "intervenes" are helpful dictionary definitions. In any event, you are entitled to relief under Rule 25 not only because your ball lies in ground under repair but also if you have to stand in it, even though the ball lies outside the area. The same applies to casual water and burrowing animal holes when the ball does not lie in a water hazard.

Speaking of burrowing animal holes, a Decision provides the final words on the subject, in reply to a question asking whether relief should be granted from holes made by a dog who digs and leaves behind heaps of earth. "A burrow is a hole or tunnel in the ground made by certain animals, such as rabbits, moles, ground hogs and gophers for shelter and habitation. Thus, a burrowing animal is an animal that makes a hole in which it may live. Since a dog does not dig holes for habitation or shelter, a hole made by a dog is not a burrowing animal hole."

The extent of relief after determining the nearest point is limited to one club-length. The same is true of relief from immovable obstructions under Rule 24.

Determining "the point on the course nearest to where the ball lies" is the hardest part of applying Rule 25. It might help to think that there are three possible points to consider every time, but only one of the three is the nearest point in the sense that your ball will have traveled the shortest distance to reach that point. Once you find that point, then you get the additional one-club-length leeway.

Note that on the putting green the relief is liberal, as it allows you to lift, move and *place* the ball to avoid intervention by casual water. However, if the ball is not on the putting green, you can complain, but that's all. Thus, if your ball is just off the green, not interfered with by casual water although there's a puddle on your line, you get no relief.

Remember that there is no such thing, by Definition, as casual water in a water hazard—but there may be casual water in a bunker.

Here are some common ground-under-repair situations:

• A player has a bad lie in ground under repair and wants to drop within the ground under repair.

Answer: He can't do it; he must drop on ground that avoids the condition—that is, outside the ground under repair.

• A player drops outside ground under repair as per Rule 25-1, but the ball rolls back into the ground under repair. It has rolled less than one club-length and no nearer the hole. He likes the lie. May he play?

Answer: No. He must re-drop. (See Rule 20-2c.)

• A player drops outside ground under repair, but now his stance is in the ground under repair. Must he drop again?

Answer: Yes.

• What can a golfer do when a bunker is completely covered by casual water?

Answer: He may drop it in the bunker in the shallowest casual water as near as possible to the spot where the ball first lay, but not nearer the hole or outside the bunker under penalty of one stroke.

• A player's ball lay in the narrow crevice of a tree. A stroke at the ball was a physical impossibility, but when the player took his stance one of his feet was on a burrowing animal hole. Was he entitled to invoke Rule 25?

Answer: No. See Exception to Rule 25-1b.

25-2. Embedded Ball

The Rule clearly defines "closely mown area" as cut at fairway height or less. Rule 25-2 does not allow relief for balls embedded in rough. If a Committee feels conditions warrant providing relief for more than "closely mown areas," it is necessary to adopt a Local Rule which might say that relief is granted for any ball embedded through the green, and not just those in "closely mown areas."

25-3. Wrong Putting Green

You may not play from a wrong putting green, including a practice green. The Rule calls for a drop within one club-length of the nearest point, no nearer the hole. This invariably allows for a drop on a beautifully groomed apron, which makes golf-course superintendents wince, but there it is.

RULE 26

WATER HAZARDS (INCLUDING LATERAL WATER HAZARDS)

A "water hazard" is any sea, lake, pond, river, ditch, surface drainage ditch or other open water course (whether or not containing water) and anything of a similar nature.

All ground or water within the margin of a water hazard is part of the water hazard. The margin of a water hazard is

Definitions

deemed to extend vertically upwards. Stakes and lines defining the margins of water hazards are in the hazards.

Note: *Water hazards (other than <u>lateral water hazards</u>) should be defined by yellow stakes or lines.*

A "lateral water hazard" is a <u>water hazard</u> or that part of a water hazard so situated that it is not possible or is deemed by the Committee to be impracticable to drop a ball behind the water hazard and keep the spot at which the ball last crossed the margin of the water hazard between the player and the hole.

That part of a water hazard to be played as a lateral water hazard should be distinctively marked.

Note: *Lateral water hazards should be defined by red stakes or lines.*

26-1
Ball in Water Hazard

It is a question of fact whether a ball lost after having been struck toward a <u>water hazard</u> is lost inside or outside the hazard. In order to treat the ball as lost in the hazard, there must be reasonable evidence that the ball lodged therein. In the absence of such evidence, the ball must be treated as a lost ball and Rule 27 applies.

If a ball lies in, touches or is lost in a water hazard (whether the ball lies in water or not), the player may *under penalty of one stroke:*

a. Play his next stroke as nearly as possible at the spot from which the original ball was last played or moved by him (see Rule 20-5);

or

b. Drop a ball behind the water hazard, keeping the point at which the original ball last crossed the margin of the water hazard directly between himself and the hole, with no limit to how far behind the water hazard the ball may be dropped;

or

c. *As additional options available only if the ball lies or is lost in a lateral water hazard,* drop a ball outside the water hazard within two club-lengths of (i) the point where the original ball last crossed the margin of the water hazard or (ii) a point on the opposite margin of the water hazard equidistant from the hole. The ball must be dropped and come to rest not nearer the hole than the point where the original ball last crossed the margin of the water hazard.

The ball may be cleaned when lifted under this Rule.

26-2
Ball Played Within Water Hazard

a. BALL REMAINS IN HAZARD

If a ball played from within a water hazard has not crossed any margin of the hazard, the player may:

(i) proceed under Rule 26-1; or

(ii) *under penalty of one stroke,* play his next stroke as nearly as possible at the spot from which the last stroke from outside the hazard was played (see Rule 20-5).

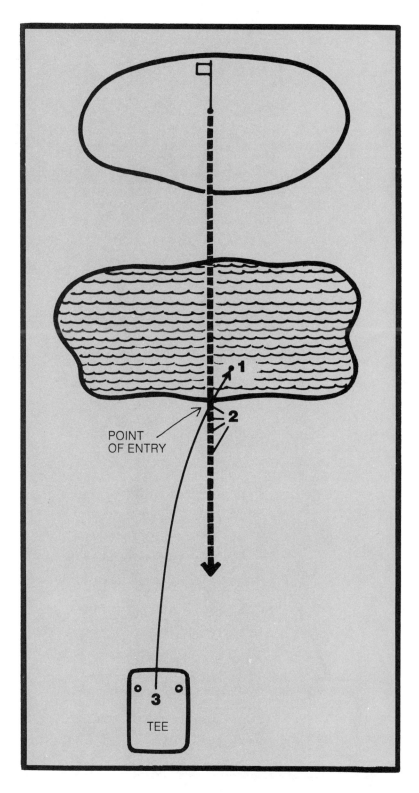

POINT
OF ENTRY

3

TEE

Water Hazard Options

You can do one of three things when your ball comes to rest in a water hazard: (1) Assuming the ball is playable, go right ahead and play it without penalty. But if it's not playable, imagine a line (2) running from the hole to the point where the ball last crossed the margin of the hazard. You can drop on an extension of that line for a penalty of one stroke. The third option (3) is stroke-and-distance. In this illustration, that means returning to the tee, where your next stroke would be your third. Note that you can't drop along the line of the ball's flight. (R. 26-1)

Lateral Water Hazard Options

There are five options when a ball lies within a lateral water hazard. Three are the same as those for a water hazard: (1) Play the ball as it lies without penalty. (2) Drop behind the hazard on a line formed by the hole and point (A) where the ball entered the hazard with a one-stroke penalty added. (3) Use the stroke-and-distance option. The other two options also call for a penalty stroke. You may drop within two club-lengths of A, no nearer the hole (4) or on the opposite size of the hazard (5). The reference point on the opposite side is B, which is the same distance from the hole as A. (R. 26-1)

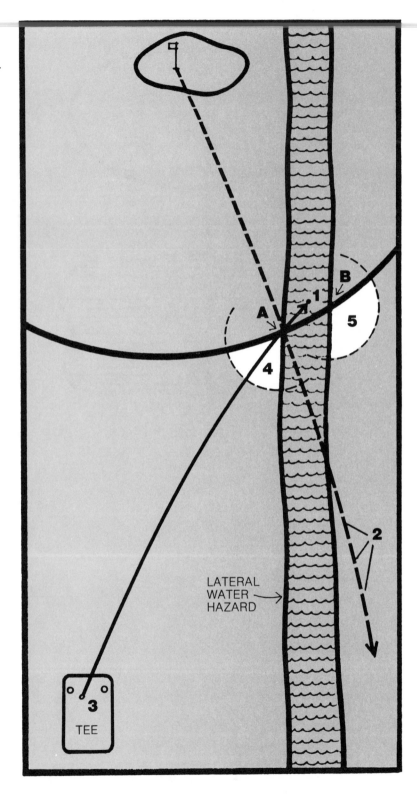

LATERAL
WATER →
HAZARD

TEE

b. Ball Lost or Unplayable Outside Hazard or Out of Bounds

If a ball played from within a water hazard is lost or declared unplayable outside the hazard or is out of bounds, the player, after taking a stroke-and-distance penalty under Rule 27-1 or 28a, may:

(i) play a ball as nearly as possible at the spot from which the original ball was last played by him (see Rule 20-5); or

(ii) under the penalty prescribed therein, proceed under Rule 26-1b or, as additional options in the case of a lateral water hazard, under Rule 26-1c, using as the reference point the point where the ball last crossed the margin of the hazard before it came to rest in the hazard; or

(iii) *under penalty of one stroke,* play his next stroke as nearly as possible at the spot from which the last stroke from outside the hazard was played (see Rule 20-5).

Penalty for Breach of Rule:

Match play—Loss of hole; Stroke play—Two strokes.

The provisions of the Rules covering water hazards in 1984 are essentially as they were before, with one modification. It often happens that a player makes a stroke within a water hazard and knocks his ball to a position in the hazard where he cannot play it.

When he drops where the original ball was played, it may roll into deep water and become unplayable. The only other option that was previously available to him, dropping behind the hazard, might not be feasible because the area behind the hazard could be covered by shrubbery or out of bounds.

To keep the player alive in stroke play, the 1984 Rules add another option in that situation. The player, under penalty of one stroke, can drop at the spot from which the last stroke from outside the water hazard was played.

Here are some keys to the application of Rule 26:

• When dropping outside a water hazard or lateral water hazard, the options do not include dropping along the "line of flight."

• Fundamental, but worth affirming: If your ball is in the water hazard and can't be found, is unplayable or you opt not to play it, the penalty is one stroke. Thus if you drive into a water hazard and drop a ball behind the hazard, your next stroke is your third.

• You may not treat a ball as being lost in a hazard just because it might be in the hazard. There must be "reasonable evidence," which is clarified in a Decision:

"The term 'reasonable evidence' in Rule 26-1 is purposely and necessarily broad so as to permit sensible judgments to be reached on the basis of all the relevant circumstances of particular cases. As applied in this context, a player may not deem his ball lost in a water hazard simply because he thinks the ball may be in the hazard. The evidence must be preponderantly in favor of its being in the hazard. Otherwise, the ball must be considered lost outside the hazard and the player must proceed under Rule 27-1. Physical conditions in the area have a great deal to do with it. For example, if a water hazard is surrounded by a fairway on which a ball could hardly be lost, the

123

existence of reasonable evidence that the ball is in the hazard would be more likely than if there was deep rough in the area. Observing a ball splash in a water hazard would not necessarily provide reasonable evidence, as splashing balls sometimes skip out of hazards."

RULE 27

BALL LOST OR OUT OF BOUNDS; PROVISIONAL BALL

If the original ball is lost under a condition covered by Rule 25-1 (casual water, ground under repair and certain damage to the course), the player may proceed under that Rule. If the original ball is lost in a water hazard, the player shall proceed under Rule 26.

Such Rules may not be used unless there is reasonable evidence that the ball is lost under a condition covered by Rule 25-1 or in a water hazard.

Definitions

A ball is "lost" if:

a. It is not found or identified as his by the player within five minutes after the player's side or his or their caddies have begun to search for it; or

b. The player has put another ball into play under the Rules, even though he may not have searched for the original ball; or

c. The player has played any stroke with a provisional ball from the place where the original ball is likely to be or from a point nearer the hole than that place, whereupon the provisional ball becomes the ball in play.

Time spent in playing a wrong ball is not counted in the five-minute period allowed for search.

"Out of bounds" is ground on which play is prohibited.

When out of bounds is defined by reference to stakes or a fence, or as being beyond stakes or a fence, the out of bounds line is determined by the nearest inside points of the stakes or fence posts at ground level excluding angled supports.

When out of bounds is fixed by a line on the ground, the line itself is out of bounds.

The out of bounds line is deemed to extend vertically upwards and downwards.

A ball is out of bounds when all of it lies out of bounds.

A player may stand out of bounds to play a ball lying within bounds.

A "provisional ball" is a ball played under this Rule for a ball which may be lost outside a water hazard or may be out of bounds. It ceases to be a provisional ball when the Rule provides either that the player continue play with it as the ball in play or that it be abandoned.

If a ball is <u>lost</u> outside a <u>water hazard</u> or is <u>out of bounds</u>, the player shall play a ball, *under penalty of one stroke,* as nearly as possible at the spot from which the original ball was last played or moved by him (see Rule 20-5).

a. PROCEDURE

If a ball may be <u>lost</u> outside a <u>water hazard</u> or may be <u>out of bounds</u>, to save time the player may play another ball provisionally as nearly as possible from the spot at which the original ball was played (see Rule 20-5). The player shall inform his opponent in match play or his marker or a fellow-competitor in stroke play that he intends to play a <u>provisional ball</u>, and he shall play it before he or his partner goes forward to search for the original ball. If he fails to do so and plays another ball, such ball is not a provisional ball and becomes the <u>ball in play</u> *under penalty of stroke and distance* (Rule 27-1); the original ball is deemed to be lost.

b. WHEN PROVISIONAL BALL BECOMES BALL IN PLAY

The player may play a provisional ball until he reaches the place where the original ball is likely to be. If he plays a stroke with the provisional ball from the place where the original ball is likely to be or from a point nearer the hole than that place, the original ball is deemed to be <u>lost</u> and the provisional ball becomes the ball in play *under penalty of stroke and distance* (Rule 27-1).

If the original ball is lost outside a water hazard or is out of bounds, the provisional ball becomes the ball in play, *under penalty of stroke and distance* (Rule 27-1).

c. WHEN PROVISIONAL BALL TO BE ABANDONED

If the original ball is neither lost outside a water hazard nor out of bounds, the player shall abandon the provisional ball and continue play with the original ball. If he fails to do so, any further strokes played with the provisional ball shall constitute playing a <u>wrong ball</u> and the provisions of Rule 15 shall apply.

Note: *If the original ball lies in a water hazard, the player shall play the ball as it lies or proceed under Rule 26. If it is lost in a water hazard or unplayable, the player shall proceed under Rule 26 or 28, whichever is applicable.*

PENALTY FOR BREACH OF RULE:
Match play—Loss of hole; Stroke play—Two strokes.

27-1
Ball Lost or Out of Bounds

27-2
Provisional Ball

Here we have the despised stroke-and-distance penalty, which means that when you knock your tee shot out of bounds (or lose it outside a water hazard), your next stroke is played from the tee again and is your third, not your second. In other words, you not only lose the distance the ball traveled but have to tack on a penalty stroke as well.

Why? Because otherwise an element of farce would be introduced into the game. Everyone agrees that the concept of allowing for the play of a provisional ball for a ball that may be lost or out of bounds is sound in that it saves time and trouble. If the penalty was to be distance only (so that the next stroke from the tee after a ball hit out of bounds counted as the second stroke), we would use the provisional not only as a timesaver but as a "Mulligan," a possible means of getting completely off the hook for playing a bad shot.

Take the par-3 4th hole at the Augusta National Golf Club. It's a hard hole with an impenetrable thicket of cane growth far to the right of the green. If I hit a ball into those canes, I've played an absolutely awful shot. It's not out of bounds and I might have to declare the ball unplayable. There's no way I can make a par and I might well make a 5 or even worse. But suppose Rule 27 were relaxed. Since the ball in the thicket might be lost, I'd be entitled to and would play a provisional ball. Let's say I play this one correctly and knock it eight feet from the hole. I would be tempted not to search for my original ball and instead march right up to the green and have a fifty-fifty chance of salvaging my par. It would be ludicrous for the Rules to allow situations to develop in which it would sometimes be in the player's best interest to lose his ball.

As a matter of fact, the "distance only" penalty was given a try in 1960 by the USGA in what were labeled "Trial Rules." They were quickly abandoned.

All right, you say, but why does it have to be both stroke *and* distance? If a ball goes out of bounds, why not drop a ball within two club-lengths of the point where the ball crossed the boundary instead of having to go all the way back? First of all, it's very hard to determine exactly where a ball goes out of bounds. Moreover, logic demands that the lost ball and out-of-bounds situations may be linked. Wild shots are commonly hit in the direction of boundaries but the ball isn't found. The ball might be out of bounds, but on the other hand it might just as well be lost in the woods on the course. Since there's no way of knowing for sure where the ball is, the only equitable resolution is a Rule in which it doesn't matter whether the ball is out of bounds or lost.

27-2. Provisional Ball

Rule 27-2 is a welcome timesaver. Although the language of the Rule seems clear enough, it is often violated by golfers who seem to think they can play provisional balls whenever the original ball might be in any sort of difficulty.

Here are the pitfalls:

• Beware of getting mixed up with water hazards. Let us assume that a ball is driven toward a water hazard flanked by trees and heavy rough. A provisional ball may be played, since the ball may be lost outside the hazard. But if the original ball is found within the hazard, the provisional ball must be abandoned and play continued as if no provisional ball existed.

• Moreover, hear this: If a player plays what he erroneously terms a "provisional ball" from the tee only because his original might be in a water hazard, the second ball from the tee is in play, since it was *not* a provisional ball—i.e., a ball that may be lost outside a water hazard or out of bounds.

• When a provisional ball is played because the original may be lost, but the original is found in an unplayable position, the provisional, like it or not, must be abandoned, and play proceeds under Rule 28, which covers unplayable situations.

● Rule 27-2 insists that the player who intends to play a provisional ball announce his intention. If a ball is driven in the direction of a boundary and the unhappy player says nothing or grunts a sound indicating dissatisfaction before driving a second ball, that second ball becomes the ball in play; the original ball, even if it's found on the course, must be abandoned. The player lies 3. The same applies to vague statements such as "I think I better reload," which is not acceptable as an announcement of intention to play a provisional ball.

RULE 28

BALL UNPLAYABLE

At any place on the course except in a water hazard a player may declare his ball unplayable. The player is the sole judge as to whether his ball is unplayable.

If the player deems his ball to be unplayable, he shall, *under penalty of one stroke:*

    a. Play his next stroke as nearly as possible at the spot from which the original ball was last played or moved by him (see Rule 20-5);

or

    b. Drop a ball within two club-lengths of the spot where the ball lay, but not nearer the hole;

or

    c. Drop a ball behind the spot where the ball lay, keeping that spot directly between himself and the hole, with no limit to how far behind that spot the ball may be dropped.

If the unplayable ball lies in a bunker and the player elects to proceed under Clause b or c, a ball must be dropped in the bunker.

The ball may be cleaned when lifted under this Rule.

PENALTY FOR BREACH OF RULE:
Match play—Loss of hole; Stroke play—Two strokes.

The USGA says it gets as much flak on one aspect of Rule 28 as on any other Rule. This seems to result from the general failure to understand that when a ball in a bunker is declared unplayable, the player may avail himself of the stroke-and-distance penalty. The ball may indeed be removed from the bunker and returned to the spot from which the ball was played into the bunker. You can always invoke the stroke-and-distance penalty.

Rule 28 Decisions include these:

● A player's ball bounced off a rock and rebounded behind him in the woods. He declared it unplayable and elected to drop at the original lie. His opponent protested, claiming that the player was advancing the ball toward the hole without playing a stroke. Who was right?

Unplayable Lie Options

You have three choices when you declare a ball unplayable through the green: (1) Go back and play from the spot where the previous stroke was played, (2) Drop a ball within two club-lengths of the spot where the ball was declared unplayable, no nearer the hole, as shown by the white area, or (3) Imagine a line from the hole to the ball and drop back on an extension of that line. In each instance there's a penalty of one stroke. If the ball is unplayable in a bunker, the stroke-and-distance option (1) is still available. Options 2 and 3, however, are modified to the extent that the ball must be dropped within the bunker if either option is used. (R. 28)

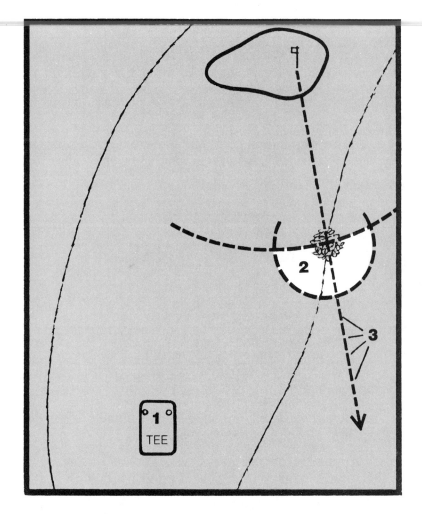

Answer: The player was entitled to drop at the original lie under the "stroke and distance" option, even though, in this rare instance, he gained rather than lost distance.

● How do you proceed when a ball is unplayable in a tree?

Answer: You determine the spot directly beneath the ball in the tree and then use Rule 28 just as if the ball were unplayable on the ground at that spot.

I still wince when I think what happened to Billy Ziobro, now the pro at the Salem Country Club near Boston, during a Hawaiian Open some years ago. I was watching from the window of a hotel adjoining the course. I saw his ball disappear in the foliage of a palm tree. Everyone was sure his ball had lodged in the palm tree, since it was apparent that the ball had entered the tree but hadn't dropped out. There was no rough in sight and, in addition, many spectators were in the area. Billy couldn't climb the tree to identify his ball and had to take the stroke-and-distance penalty for a lost ball instead of declaring the ball unplayable and dropping near the base of the tree for a penalty of one stroke.

OTHER FORMS OF PLAY

RULE 29

THREESOMES AND FOURSOMES

Threesome: A match in which one plays against two, and each side plays one ball.

Foursome: A match in which two play against two, and each side plays one ball.

In a threesome or a foursome, during any <u>stipulated round</u> the partners shall play alternately from the <u>teeing grounds</u> and alternately during the play of each hole. <u>Penalty strokes</u> do not affect the order of play.

If a player plays when his partner should have played, *his side shall lose the hole.*

If the partners play a stroke or strokes in incorrect order, such stroke or strokes shall be canceled and *the side shall be penalized two strokes.* A ball shall then be put in play as nearly as possible at the spot from which the side first played in incorrect order (see Rule 20-5) before a stroke has been played from the next <u>teeing ground</u> or, in the case of the last hole of the round, before the side has left the <u>putting green</u>. If this is not done, *the side shall be disqualified.*

Rule 29 is almost never referred to in the United States, because a threesome is virtually an extinct form of play and we very seldom play foursomes.

Remember what the Definition says: A threesome is not what hap-

129

pens when three golfers play together. It's a form of play in which one plays against two, and each side plays one ball; that is, the team of two plays alternate strokes with one ball. A foursome is not what happens when four golfers play together; it's a form of competition in which two play against two with each side using one ball, playing alternate strokes.

At the great Muirfield Course in Scotland, home of the Honourable Company of Edinburgh Golfers, there's a venerable tradition concerning foursomes which I think should be tried, at least occasionally, at American clubs.

At Muirfield nothing except foursomes play is permitted on weekend mornings. A brisk foursome, which might have one partner already in the drive zones on many holes waiting to play the second shot for his team, can be played in two and a half hours.

Then comes lunch, and perhaps a four-ball match played in another three and a half hours. All told, the member gets in 36 holes and lunch (with a stupefying drink named Kimmel) in less than seven hours—an estimable goal for all of us.

RULE 30

THREE-BALL, BEST-BALL AND FOUR-BALL MATCH PLAY

30-1

Rules of Golf Apply

The Rules of Golf, so far as they are not at variance with the following special Rules, shall apply to three-ball, best-ball and four-ball matches.

30-2

Three-Ball Match Play

In a three-ball match, each player is playing two distinct matches.

a. BALL AT REST MOVED BY AN OPPONENT

Except as otherwise provided in the Rules, if the player's ball is touched or moved by an opponent, his caddie or equipment other than during search, Rule 18-3b applies. *That opponent shall incur a penalty stroke in his match with the player,* but not in his match with the other opponent.

b. BALL DEFLECTED OR STOPPED BY AN OPPONENT ACCIDENTALLY

If a player's ball is accidentally deflected or stopped by an opponent, his caddie or equipment, no penalty shall be incurred. In his match with that opponent the player may play the ball as it lies or, before another stroke is played by either side, he may cancel the stroke and replay the stroke (see Rule 20-5). In his match with the other opponent, the occurrence shall be treated as a rub of the green and the hole shall be played out with the original ball.

Exception: Ball striking person attending flagstick—Rule 17-3b.

(Ball purposely deflected or stopped by opponent—Rule 19-3a.)

a. REPRESENTATION OF SIDE

A side may be represented by one partner for all or any part of a match; all partners need not be present. An absent partner may join a match between holes, but not during play of a hole.

b. MAXIMUM OF FOURTEEN CLUBS

The side shall be penalized for a breach of Rule 4-4 by any partner.

c. ORDER OF PLAY

Balls belonging to the same side may be played in the order the side considers best.

d. WRONG BALL

If a player plays a stroke with a <u>wrong ball</u> except in a <u>hazard</u>, *he shall be disqualified for that hole,* but his partner incurs no penalty even if the wrong ball belongs to him. The owner of the ball shall replace it on the spot from which it was played, without penalty. If the ball is not immediately recoverable, another ball may be substituted.

e. DISQUALIFICATION OF SIDE

(i) *A side shall be disqualified* for a breach of any of the following by any partner:

Rule 1-3—Agreement to Waive Rules.
Rule 4-1, -2 or -3—Clubs.
Rule 5—The Ball.
Rule 6-2a—Handicap (playing off higher handicap).
Rule 6-4—Caddie.
Rule 6-7—Undue Delay (repeated offense).
Rule 14-3—Artificial Devices and Unusual Equipment

(ii) *A side shall be disqualified* for a breach of any of the following by all partners:

Rule 6-3—Time of Starting and Groups.
Rule 6-8—Discontinuance of Play.

f. EFFECT OF OTHER PENALTIES

If a player's breach of a Rule assists his partner's play or adversely affects an opponent's play, *the partner incurs the relative penalty in addition to any penalty incurred by the player.*

In all other cases where a player incurs a penalty for breach of a Rule, the penalty shall not apply to his partner. Where the penalty is stated to be loss of hole, the effect shall be to disqualify the player for that hole.

g. ANOTHER FORM OF MATCH PLAYED CONCURRENTLY

In a best-ball or four-ball match when another form of match is played concurrently, the above special Rules shall apply.

30-3
Best-Ball and Four-Ball Match Play

The most popular form of play is undoubtedly four-ball match play, which consists of two playing their better ball on each hole against the better ball of two others.

Rule 30 also covers Best-Ball (when one player goes up against the best ball of either two or three others) and Three-Ball (when three play against one another, each playing his own ball). But these two

Four-Ball Match Play

In a four-ball match, any player can have any ball lifted before a stroke is made. In this illustration, A and B are partners and it's A's turn to putt. He'll surely require that C's ball be lifted, since it's on his line. A would probably like B's ball to stay right where it is, since it could serve as a useful backstop, but either C or D can require B to lift his ball. As for ball D, it's off the line of putt, but A can have it lifted if it bothers him. If any ball is not lifted and is struck by ball A, there is no penalty. A would play from where his ball then lies, while the owner of the displaced ball, whether he's A's partner or opponent, must replace it. (R. 30)

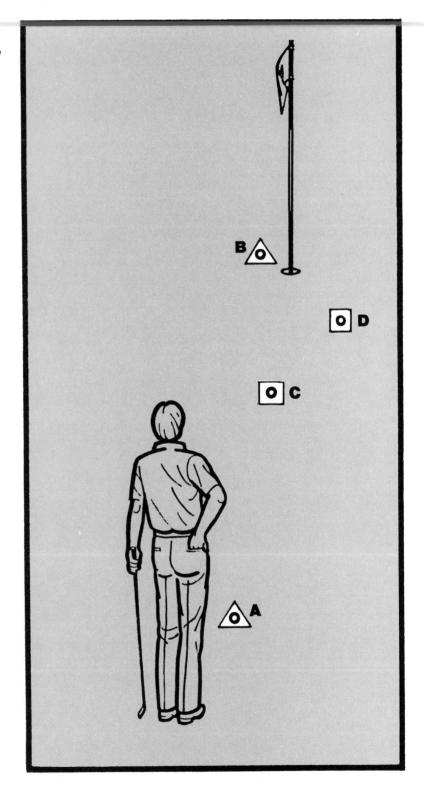

forms of play are so rare that we'll skip them and concentrate on four-ball match play.

Let's go right to the site of common confusion—on the putting green: In four-ball match, good old A and B are up against C and D.

CASE 1: A is away and B's ball is inches beyond the hole in such a position that it might very well assist A as a backstop. Mr. A would like B's ball to stay right where it is, but back in Rule 22 we learned that C and D have the right to require that B's ball be lifted.

CASE 2: This time B's ball is directly in front of the hole on A's line. Naturally, A and B want B's ball lifted and they may do so.

CASE 3: Now picture C's ball just beyond the hole where it might help A. C can mark and lift his ball.

CASE 4: C's ball is on A's line. A can require him to lift it.

Let's assume, however, that in each case no ball is marked, that A putts and strikes the ball of either B, his partner, or C, his opponent. There is no penalty. A plays from where his ball then lies. The owner of the ball moved, be it partner or opponent, must replace his ball.

Singles matches are often played concurrently with the four-ball match. Thus A and B are not only going up against the team of C and D, but A is waging singles matches at the same time against C and D, and sometimes even against partner B. What to do when the procedure for four-ball match play is at variance with those for single matches? Easy. The four-ball rules have priority! It says so loud and clear in Rule 30-3g.

Some other key elements in four-ball matches:

• Rule 30-3c introduces a strategic possibility in that even though A is away, his partner—Dr. B.—may play first. Then it's A's turn.

• When your ball is deflected by your partner, caddie or equipment (including a cart you may be sharing), you are disqualified for that hole, but your partner is not.

• When your ball is accidentally deflected by one of your opponents, their caddies or their equipment, there is no penalty. You have a choice of either playing your ball as it lies or replaying the stroke.

• When a player violates a Rule, his partner is not penalized unless the nature of the violation is such that it helps his partner or hurts the play of an opponent. When that happens, both members of the team are penalized. Example: After balls have been lifted and replaced on a putting green, A makes a mistake and putts from the spot where B's marker was. The putt is a tricky downhiller, with a big right-to-left break. A, having played from the wrong place, is disqualified on that hole, and B, since he might very well have been assisted by observing the roll of the ball, should also be disqualified.

There is one change of consequence in the Rules for four-ball play, effective in 1984. If one partner is late, or even if he never shows up, his partner alone can play the other team. If the missing partner shows up, he can join the match in progress, but only at the start of any hole.

The Rules used to say that when a player was late he was disqualified from that match. The Committee then had to decide whether or not to allow his partner play the other team alone or, alternatively, to forfeit the match.

RULE 31

FOUR-BALL STROKE PLAY

In four-ball stroke play two competitors play as partners, each playing his own ball. The lower score of the partners is the score for the hole. If one partner fails to complete the play of a hole, there is no penalty.

31-1
Rules of Golf Apply

The Rules of Golf, so far as they are not at variance with the following special Rules, shall apply to four-ball stroke play.

31-2
Representation of Side

A side may be represented by either partner for all or any part of a stipulated round; both partners need not be present. An absent competitor may join his partner between holes, but not during play of a hole.

31-3
Maximum of Fourteen Clubs

The side shall be penalized for a breach of Rule 4-4 by either partner.

31-4
Scoring

The marker is required to record for each hole only the gross score of whichever partner's score is to count. The gross scores to count must be individually identifiable; otherwise *the side shall be disqualified.* Only one of the partners need be responsible for complying with Rule 6-6a and b.
(Wrong score—Rule 31-7a.)

31-5
Order of Play

Balls belonging to the same side may be played in the order the side considers best.

31-6
Wrong Ball

If a competitor plays a stroke with a wrong ball except in a hazard, *he shall add two penalty strokes to his score for the hole* and shall then play the correct ball. His partner incurs no penalty even if the wrong ball belongs to him.
The owner of the ball shall replace it on the spot from which it was played, without penalty. If the ball is not immediately recoverable, another ball may be substituted.

31-7
Disqualification Penalties

a. BREACH BY ONE PARTNER
A side shall be disqualified from the competition for a breach of any of the following by either partner:
Rule 1-3—Agreement to Waive Rules.
Rule 3-4—Refusal to Comply with Rule.
Rule 4-1, -2 or -3—Clubs.
Rule 5—The Ball.
Rule 6-2b—Handicap (playing off higher handicap; failure to record handicap).

Rule 6-4—Caddie.

Rule 6-6b—Checking Scores.

Rule 6-6c—No Alteration of Scores, *i.e.,* when the recorded lower score of the partners is lower than actually played. If the recorded lower score of the partners is higher than actually played, it must stand as returned.

Rule 6-7—Undue Delay (repeated offense).

Rule 7-1—Practice Before or Between Rounds.

Rule 14-3—Artificial Devices and Unusual Equipment

Rule 31-4—Gross Scores to Count Not Individually Identifiable

b. BREACH BY BOTH PARTNERS

A side shall be disqualified for a breach of any of the following by both partners:

Rule 6-3—Time of Starting and Groups.

Rule 6-8—Discontinuance of Play.

At the same hole, of a Rule or Rules, the penalty for which is disqualification either from the competition or for a hole.

c. FOR THE HOLE ONLY

In all other cases where a breach of a Rule would entail disqualification, *the competitor shall be disqualified only for the hole at which the breach occurred.*

If a competitor's breach of a Rule assists his partner's play, *the partner incurs the relative penalty in addition to any penalty incurred by the competitor.*

In all other cases where a competitor incurs a penalty for breach of a Rule, the penalty shall not apply to his partner.

31-8
Effect of Other Penalties

The Rules governing four-ball stroke and four-ball match play differ when a ball is moved by another ball. In four-ball stroke play, when a ball is putted from the putting area and strikes another ball on the green, the player who putted is penalized two strokes. The moved ball must be replaced.

Partners in four-ball stroke play may not "use" each other's balls as potential backstops. If A is about to play from a bunker and the ball of partner B is just beyond the hole, B's ball should be removed.

A and B should handle this detail by themselves, but if they are careless, the fellow-competitors, C and D, should have B's ball lifted —in fairness to the rest of the field.

Rule 31 is customarily adopted to control best-ball-of-four competitions—those in which each four-man team counts the best score on a hole as the team score for the hole. Another standard variation is the pro-amateur format, which finds the pro recording his score on each hole (since he's playing a stroke play competition against the other pros in the field) while at the same time engaging his amateur partners in a best-ball-of-four (or even five) competition.

Bogey, Par and Stableford Competitions

32-1
Conditions

Bogey, par and Stableford competitions are forms of stroke competition in which play is against a fixed score at each hole. The Rules for stroke play, so far as they are not at variance with the following special Rules, apply.

a. BOGEY AND PAR COMPETITIONS

The reckoning for bogey and par competitions is made as in match play. Any hole for which a competitor makes no return shall be regarded as a loss. The winner is the competitor who is most successful in the aggregate of holes.

The marker is responsible for marking only the gross number of strokes for each hole where the competitor makes a net score equal to or less than the fixed score.

Note: *Maximum of 14 clubs—Penalties as in match play— see Rule 4-4.*

b. STABLEFORD COMPETITIONS

The reckoning in Stableford competitions is made by points awarded in relation to a fixed score at each hole as follows:

Hole Played In	Points
More than one over fixed score	0
One over fixed score	1
Fixed score	2
One under fixed score	3
Two under fixed score	4
Three under fixed score	5

The winner is the competitor who scores the highest number of points.

The marker shall be responsible for marking only the gross number of strokes at each hole where the competitor's net score earns one or more points.

Note: *Maximum of 14 clubs (Rule 4-4)—Penalties applied as follows: From total points scored for the round, deduction of two points for each hole at which any breach occurred; maximum deduction per round: four points.*

32-2
Disqualification Penalties

a. FROM THE COMPETITION

A competitor shall be disqualified from the competition for a breach of any of the following:

Rule 1-3—Agreement to Waive Rules.

Rule 3-4—Refusal to Comply with Rule.

Rule 4-1, -2 or -3—Clubs.

Rule 5—The Ball.

Rule 6-2b—Handicap (playing off higher handicap; failure to record handicap).

Rule 6-3—Time of Starting and Groups.

Rule 6-4—Caddie.

Rule 6-6b—Checking Scores.

Rule 6-6c—No alteration of scores, except that the competitor shall not be disqualified when a breach of this Rule does not affect the result of the hole.

Rule 6-7—Undue Delay (repeated offense).

Rule 6-8—Discontinuance of Play.

Rule 7-1—Practice Before or Between Rounds.

Rule 14-3—Artificial Devices and Unusual Equipment.

b. FOR A HOLE

In all other cases where a breach of a Rule would entail disqualification, *the competitor shall be disqualified only for the hole at which the breach occurred.*

Rule 32 sets down the conditions for some forms of competition that offer a form of relief from the routine of standard stroke play.

Bogey or Par competitions are played against a fixed score. The most popular method calls for the par on each hole to serve as the opponent. A player competes against par with the help of a handicap. The winner is the player who is most ahead of par after eighteen holes.

Stableford competitions are indigenous to Great Britain. They're often called "point" tournaments here. They're a lot of fun because they allow players of every level of skill to play, suffer and exult together. A common form of Stableford sends out teams of four, each player using full handicap. A net score of a double bogey, or worse, for a player earns no points on a hole, but a bogey is worth 1 point, a par 2 points and so on up to 5 points on a hole for a net double eagle. The winning team is the one that amasses the most total points. Every two-foot putt for a net bogey takes on a meaning all its own.

Stableford, in case you're interested, was Dr. Frank B. Stableford of Great Britain, a surgeon and first-rate golfer who invented the scoring system that bears his name. History records that the first Stableford tournament was played on May 16, 1932, on the Wallasey Links, Cheshire, England.

ADMINISTRATION

RULE 33

THE COMMITTEE

33-1
Conditions

The Committee shall lay down the conditions under which a competition is to be played.

Certain special rules governing stroke play are so substantially different from those governing match play that combining the two forms of play is not practicable and is not permitted. The results of matches played and the scores returned in these circumstances shall not be accepted.

In stroke play the Committee may limit a referee's duties.

33-2
The Course

a. DEFINING BOUNDS AND MARGINS
The Committee shall define accurately:
   (i) the <u>course</u> and <u>out of bounds</u>,
   (ii) the margins of <u>water hazards</u> and <u>lateral water hazards</u>,
   (iii) <u>ground under repair</u>, and
   (iv) <u>obstructions</u> and integral parts of the course.
b. NEW HOLES
New holes should be made on the day on which a stroke competition begins and at such other times as the Committee considers necessary, provided all competitors in a single round play with each hole cut in the same position.
Exception: When it is impossible for a damaged hole to be repaired so that it conforms with the Definition, the Committee may make a new hole in a nearby similar position.
c. PRACTICE GROUND
Where there is no practice ground available outside the area of a competition <u>course</u>, the Committee should lay down the area on which players may practice on any day of a competition, if it is practicable to do so. On any day of a stroke

competition, the Committee should not normally permit practice on or to a <u>putting green</u> or from a <u>hazard</u> of the competition course.

d. COURSE UNPLAYABLE

If the Committee or its authorized representative considers
that for any reason the course is not in a playable condition
or that there are circumstances which render the proper playing of the game impossible, it may, in match play or stroke
play, order a temporary suspension of play or, in stroke
play, declare play null and void and cancel all scores for the round
in question. When play has been temporarily suspended, it
shall be resumed from where it was discontinued, even
though resumption occurs on a subsequent day. When a
round is canceled, all penalties incurred in that round are
canceled.

(Procedure in discontinuing play—Rule 6-8.)

33-3
Times of Starting and Groups

The Committee shall lay down the times of starting and, in
stroke play, arrange the groups in which competitors shall
play.

When a match play competition is played over an extended
period, the Committee shall lay down the limit of time within
which each round shall be completed. When players are allowed to arrange the date of their match within these limits,
the Committee should announce that the match must be
played at a stated time on the last day of the period unless the
players agree to a prior date.

33-4
Handicap Stroke Table

The Committee shall publish a table indicating the order of
holes at which handicap strokes are to be given or received.

33-5
Score Card

In stroke play, the Committee shall issue for each competitor a score card containing the date and the competitor's
name.

The Committee is responsible for the addition of scores
and application of the handicap recorded on the card.

In four-ball stroke play, the Committee is responsible for
recording the better ball score for each hole, the addition and
the application of the handicaps recorded on the card.

33-6
Decision of Ties

The Committee shall announce the manner, day and time
for the decision of a halved match or of a tie, whether played
on level terms or under handicap.

A halved match shall not be decided by stroke play. A tie in
stroke play shall not be decided by a match.

33-7
Modification of Penalty

The Committee has no power to waive a Rule of Golf. A
penalty of disqualification, however, may, in exceptional individual cases, be waived or be modified or be imposed if the
Committee considers such action warranted.

139

33-8

Local Rules

a. POLICY

The Committee may make and publish Local Rules for abnormal conditions if they are consistent with the policy of the Governing Authority for the country concerned as set forth in Appendix I to these Rules.

b. WAIVING PENALTY

A penalty imposed by a Rule of Golf shall not be waived by a Local Rule.

Rule 33 is addressed to those in charge of a competition—the Committee—rather than to the player, but it behooves every golfer to know what Rule 33 is all about. Those who serve on Committees at any level of play should know it inside out. Here's an analysis of each part of Rule 33.

33-1. General

The conditions should be spelled out in the finest detail. They include the form of play, who is eligible to enter, the number of players in the field, the schedule of rounds, and prizes.

The second paragraph points out that match and stroke play are like oil and water. Golfers nevertheless go right on attempting to play matches during a stroke-play round. They run up against conflicts such as the elementary one that occurs when a ball not "away" is played. In match play, the opponent can recall that stroke; in stroke play, there is no penalty.

33-2. The Course

I recognize that it's difficult for Committees to keep courses marked properly for everyday play—particularly with respect to the margins of water hazards and ground under repair—but the effort should be made.

When water hazards are not defined and players have to sort things out for themselves, they should bear in mind that the natural limit of the hazard is considered the spot where the ground breaks down to form the depression containing the water. That's where lines and stakes defining the limits of water hazards should normally be placed.

The Committee's powers and limitations with respect to suspending play or canceling a round are spelled out in Rule 33-2d.

In match play, all a Committee can do is suspend play and decide when play is to be resumed. Once a match starts and the course becomes unplayable, the results of the holes played before suspension of play are to stand as recorded. Any strokes taken on a hole not completed count. Play is resumed where the ball lay at the time of suspension. The match is never begun anew on the first tee.

In stroke play the Committee can, at its discretion, either cancel an entire round or rule that play is to be resumed where it was discontinued—even on a later day. As a general rule of thumb, the USGA thinks that it's reasonable for a Committee to cancel an entire round when less than half the field completes or could complete play on the day in question. On the PGA Tour, our Committee seldom cancels a round once play has started. The point is that Committees are all-powerful in this regard, and they have different priorities. What's best for the

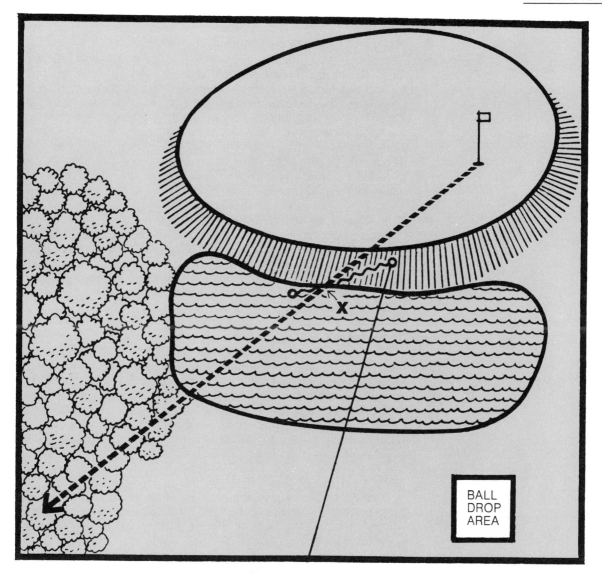

BALL
DROP
AREA

Ball-Drop Areas

Committees can install special ball-drop areas when it's impractical or unfair to limit players to the standard water hazard options. Take this hole, which has a pond directly in front of the green and a slope between the pond and the elevated green. Balls often carry beyond the hazard into the slope but then carom back into the hazard. Often dropping behind the point where the ball last entered the hazard (X) on an extension of a line between the point and the hole means the player would have to drop into a veritable jungle. The stroke-and-distance option, of course, is always available, but that seems too severe. So the Committee installs a clearly defined ball-drop area (lower right), which the player may use for the customary penalty of one stroke.

141

Tour, where it's very important to complete 72 holes by Sunday, may not be best for a club member-guest tournament.

33-3. Order and Times of Starting

Club match-play competitions are often fouled up by a failure of Committees to specify and enforce time limits for the play of rounds. The inability or unwillingness of opponents to get together for a match can spoil a tournament. One way to forestall such a delay is to assign starting times in advance to every match in every round but to allow any match to be played at another time, or even on another day, provided the match is completed prior to the time and date established for the next round.

33-4. Handicap Stroke Table

That's what every Committee does on club score cards. Clubs agonize over the order in which strokes should be allocated, but USGA mathematicians have run computer studies suggesting that it makes little or no difference over the long run on which holes the strokes are taken. What matters is that the total number of strokes between opponents be equitable.

33-5. Score Card

Score cards are required only in stroke play. In match play they are a convenience, and all that ultimately matters is that the opponents agree on the status and conclusion of the match. They are not required to sign or return a card.

The Committee bears the responsibility for addition. The player has to put in the correct numbers for each hole. If a player does his job but then fouls up the addition, he is not to worry. The Committee has to get it right.

33-6. Decision of Ties

Committees often fail to announce in advance what will happen in the event of a tie. Whenever they fail to do so, someone is invariably unhappy because the method selected after the fact always seems to favor someone else.

33-7. Modification of Penalty

Let's take a couple of examples of what this section means:

• As a condition of play, a Committee says it's okay to tamp down something it calls "spike marks." In doing so, it has waived Rule 16-1. Boo and hiss! The game is now being played under something other than the Rules of Golf.

• Rule 6-3a says that a player is to be disqualified if he arrives at the first tee late. But suppose he's about to turn into the club driveway and sees a fire in a house across the street. He stops, runs into the building and saves a child, a dog and the kid's stereo. Then he resumes his journey but shows up ten minutes late. The Committee should certainly consider waiving any penalty.

33-8. Local Rules

Before any round, the wise golfer will check the back of the score card and any other likely place, such as a bulletin board, for the posting of Local Rules. A Committee should not impose Local Rules contrary to the Rules of Golf. One bad example would be a Local Rule reading "fourteen-club rule waived."

RULE 34

DISPUTES AND DECISIONS

a. MATCH PLAY

In match play if a claim is lodged with the Committee under Rule 2-5, a decision should be given as soon as possible so that the state of the match may, if necessary, be adjusted.

If a claim is not made within the time limit provided by Rule 2-5, it shall not be considered unless it is based on facts previously unknown to the player making the claim and the player making the claim had been given wrong information (Rules 6-2a and 9) by an opponent. In any case, no later claim shall be considered after the result of the match has been officially announced, unless the Committee is satisfied that the opponent knew he was giving wrong information.

b. STROKE PLAY

No penalty shall be imposed after the competition is closed unless the Committee is satisfied that the competitor has knowingly returned a score for any hole lower than actually taken (Rule 6-6c); no penalty shall be rescinded after the competition is closed. A competition is deemed to have closed when the result of the competition is officially announced or, in stroke play qualifying followed by match play, when the player has teed off in his first match.

34-1
Claims and Penalties

If a referee has been appointed by the Committee, his decision shall be final.

34-2
Referee's Decision

In the absence of a referee, the players shall refer any dispute to the Committee, whose decision shall be final.

If the Committee cannot come to a decision, it shall refer the dispute to the Rules of Golf Committee of the United States Golf Association, whose decision shall be final.

If the point in doubt or dispute has not been referred to the Rules of Golf Committee, the player or players have the right to refer an agreed statement through the Secretary of the Club to the Rules of Golf Committee for an opinion as to the correctness of the decision given. The reply will be sent to the Secretary of the Club or Clubs concerned.

If play is conducted other than in accordance with the Rules of Golf, the Rules of Golf Committee will not give a decision on any question.

34-3
Committee's Decision

143

Rule 34 covers the sensitive area of doubts and disagreements and tells how to settle them. Each of its sections deserves careful consideration.

34-1. Claims and Penalties

Focus on the words "claim" and on "wrong information."

A claim, while there are nice and not-so-nice ways of going about it, boils down to telling your opponent that you think he has violated a Rule. In order for a claim to be valid, it must be timely. It's no good seeing him ground his club in a hazard on the 12th hole and bringing up the painful subject when you're 1 down playing the 18th. You see, the statute of limitations for the 12th hole expired when one of you drove from the 13th tee, since you witnessed the violation.

Wrong information usually has to do with the number of strokes taken. It applies to a bald-faced lie (having taken seven strokes but saying you've taken only six) and, in an application that goes right to the heart of the game, if you were not aware of the violation.

Some landmark decisions on claims:

● A pushed his tee shot into the rough and among trees on the 8th hole. After searching for three or four minutes, he found a ball on the adjoining 9th fairway. It was the same make and number as his ball. A played it and went on to win the 8th hole. After they began to play the 9th hole, a player in the group ahead of them informed A that he had played the wrong ball on the 8th hole. After examining the ball again, A discovered that he had indeed played a wrong ball. Could B claim the 8th hole retroactively?

Answer: Yes, he could. A had given wrong information by failing to inform his opponent of the violation, even though A was not aware he had played a wrong ball. This would apply anytime until the result of the match was officially announced. In club play, that means when the winner's name is posted on a score sheet.

● With his opponent B safely on in 2, A takes 3 strokes to get out of a bunker and concedes the hole. As B picks up his ball, he realizes and announces that he played a wrong ball during the play of the hole. A, although he had conceded, claims the hole.

Answer: A's claim is valid, since it was made before either player played from the next tee. He wins the hole.

● Does a player calling a violation on a hole have to cite the Rule violated, or is it good enough that he knows some Rule has been violated?

Answer: The claim must be reasonably specific and accurate, but the player calling the hole doesn't have to know the Rule's number. For instance, if A putts straddle or croquet style and B says "The Rules prohibit such a stance and I call the hole," the Committee should uphold the claim. But if B had said "I call the hole because a stroke from your stance is automatically a push," the claim should not be upheld, since a saddle-style stroke is not automatically a push.

Some stroke play incidents, under 34-1b:

On the morning after the 1977 Jackie Gleason Inverrary Classic ended, Hale Irwin was jolted by a newspaper account of the final round. He read that Grier Jones had been penalized for dropping into a special "ball drop" area after hitting his ball into a water hazard.

The Local Rule that applied to the situation said the drop area could be used only if a ball entered the hazard in a particular area. Jones had misunderstood the Rule and used the drop area even though he was not entitled to use it. Irwin realized he had done exactly the same thing. He had failed to include a two-stroke penalty on the hole in question, he had turned in a score lower than the one he actually made and he should be disqualified. He had tied for seventh and his prize was $7,375.

Irwin called Clyde Mangum, Deputy Commissioner of Tour Operations, and in effect turned himself in. He told Mangum of his error and said he considered himself disqualified and would return his check forthwith. Mangum replied that Irwin could not be penalized after the results of the tournament had been announced, since wrong information had not been given knowingly. He hadn't *knowingly* violated a Rule. Irwin was adamant. Mangum said he would not accept the check, and suggested that they call the ultimate USGA rules expert, P. J. Boatwright, who, as Mangum knew he would, told Irwin that it would be contrary to the Rules of Golf for any penalty to be invoked at that point.

If the incident had occurred *between* rounds, while the tournament was still in progress, Irwin would have been disqualified under Rule 6-6, for returning a score lower than he'd actually made. The point behind this Rule is that there must be a time when a competition is finished. Irwin happened to learn of the violation the day after it happened, but he might just as easily have learned of it on a practice putting green with Grier Jones six months later. Without a statute of limitations we'd never be certain of the outcome of a tournament.

34-2. Referee's Decision

The only time I play with a referee is when I'm in contention in the last rounds of either the U.S. or British Open Championship, the PGA Championship, or the Ryder Cup Match. In those events, referees are customarily appointed to accompany the final pairings. All my other competitive rounds are administered by representatives of the Committee (in my case the PGA Tour staff) sprinkled around the course and ready to help when needed.

34-3. Committee's Decision

Dozens of times every year, written replies to Rules questions from the USGA begin with these ominous words: "The Committee's decision was wrong. However, it was final under Rule 34-3."

It has to be that way. Someone has to be in charge to make rulings on the spot, and sometimes that someone is going to make a mistake.

At least 99 percent of golf is played informally, and most of that 99 percent is played at match play. If there is a doubt or dispute about the Rules out on the course, the players should agree on the facts and then continue the match, even though they will not then be sure of the status of the match. They should get a decision as soon as they can without delaying play. Whoever is in charge of a golf course should authorize someone to make decisions, and it makes eminently good sense for that authority to be given to the golf professional.

A NOTE ON LOCAL RULES

LOCAL RULES

It is the responsibility of the Committee to decide whether it's necessary to make Local Rules, but such Local Rules should not be contrary to the Rules of Golf.

Local Rules customarily appear on the reverse sides of score cards and are often supplemented by notices posted on bulletin boards or near the first tee.

Appendix I of the Rules of Golf booklet says, "Among the matters for which Local Rules may be advisable are the following":

1. Obstructions

Clarifying the status of objects which may be obstructions (Rule 24).

Declaring any construction to be an integral part of the course and, accordingly, not an obstruction, e.g., built-up sides and surfaces of teeing grounds, putting greens and bunkers (Rules 24 and 33-2a).

2. Roads and Paths

Providing relief of the type afforded under Rule 24-2b from roads and paths not having artificial surfaces and sides if they could unfairly affect play.

3. Preservation of Course

Preservation of the course by defining areas, including turf nurseries and other parts of the course under cultivation, as ground under repair from which play is prohibited.

4. Unusual Damage to the Course

(other than as covered in Rule 25)

5. Water Hazards

Lateral Water Hazards. Clarifying the status of sections of water hazards which may be lateral water hazards (Rule 26).

Provisional Ball. Permitting play of a provisional ball for a ball which may be in a water hazard of such character that it would be impracticable to determine whether the ball is in the hazard or to do so would unduly delay play. In such case, if a provisional ball is played and the original ball is in a water hazard, the player may play the original ball as it lies or continue the provisional ball in play, but he may not proceed under Rule 26-1.

6. Defining Bounds and Margins

Specifying means used to define out of bounds, hazards, water hazards, lateral water hazards and ground under repair.

7. Ball Drops

Establishment of special areas on which balls may be dropped when it is not feasible to proceed exactly in conformity with Rule 24-2b (immovable obstructions), Rule 26-1 (water hazards and lateral water hazards) and Rule 28 (ball unplayable).

8. Temporary Conditions—Mud, Extreme Wetness

Temporary conditions which might interfere with proper playing of the game, including mud and extreme wetness warranting lifting an embedded ball anywhere through the green (see detailed recommendation below) or removal of mud from a ball through the green.

Appendix I also suggests the text for a Local Rule authorizing lifting embedded balls "through the green" when a Committee feels that it would be unfair to confine the lifting of embedded balls to the putting green (see Rule 16-1c) and other closely mown areas (see Rule 25-2). Unless a more generous Local Rule is in effect, balls that are embedded in the rough may not be lifted without penalty.

"Preferred Lies" and "Winter Rules," which allow for moving the ball contrary to the principle expressed in Rule 13: "the ball shall be played as it lies," are also a subject in Appendix I. The USGA says it does not endorse such Rules and will not interpret them, and points out quite correctly that they do fundamental damage to the principle that the ball should be played as it lies.

At the same time, it is recognized that conditions are sometimes so harsh that it's not possible to have a decent game without some form of "Preferred Lies" or "Winter Rules."

It is essential that this condition be covered by a detailed Local Rule. A notice posted only with the wording "Winter Rules" doesn't do the job. It suggests that the lie of the ball may be improved, but it doesn't answer the fundamental questions:

• May the lie of the ball be improved only in the fairway of the hole being played, on any fairway, through the green, or in hazards—or sections of some hazards?

• When the ball is moved, may it be lifted, and if so, cleaned, or must it be moved only with a clubhead?

• How far may the ball be moved—six inches, one club-length, two club-lengths?

• When is the ball in play? Is it, for instance, in play as soon as it has been placed, or not in play until the player makes his next stroke?

The text of a Local Rule included in Appendix I reads: "A ball lying on a 'fairway' may be lifted and cleaned, without penalty, and placed within six inches of where it originally lay, not nearer the hole, and so as to preserve as nearly as possible the stance required to play from the original lie. After the ball has been so placed, it is in play, and if it moves after the player has addressed it, *the penalty shall be one stroke*—see Rule 18-2b."

RULES QUIZ

RULES QUIZ

So now you know it all! You've plowed through my admonitions on Etiquette, the Definitions, the thirty-four Rules and Local Rules.

I hope you have enjoyed your labors and have profited from them. For your final exam I have included a quiz primarily devised by the USGA's P. J. Boatwright, Jr., to test the skills of a group of golf association executives attending a conference. It's meant to test your ability to *use* this book rather than your ability to snap off the correct answers. It's very much an open-book test, and each and every answer is readily available within the Rules proper. Incidentally, the first ten questions relate to changes that took effect in 1984.

The best way to join in the challenge of this quiz is to try to answer as many questions as possible within thirty minutes.

It is not intended to be an easy quiz. Anything but! If you can answer 40 of the 50 questions correctly within the thirty minutes, you're not far from being an expert. Anything better than that and you are one already! Good luck, and thanks for being an interested student.

The answers to the quiz appear on page 163.

1. It's a stroke play tournament and there's a wait on the first tee. A player in the next group to start passes time by chipping a couple of balls onto the tee. Which is correct?

_____(a) He incurs a one-stroke penalty.

_____(b) The player is disqualified.

_____(c) No penalty.

_____(d) He incurs a two-stroke penalty.

2. There is a high school competition, at stroke play, and prizes will be awarded to the teams and the individuals with the lowest scores. A coach perches on the tee of a par-3 hole and each member of his team asks him about club selection on that hole. What's the ruling?

_____(a) No penalty.

_____(b) Each player is penalized one stroke.

_____(c) Each player is penalized two strokes.

_____(d) The team is disqualified.

3. In a fairway during a four-ball match, Player A, who was away, plays first. His partner, B, then plays even though he's closer to the hole than either of their opponents. What can the opponents do?

_____(a) Nothing. There's no penalty.

_____(b) Properly claim the hole.

_____(c) Require B to replay his stroke.

_____(d) Require both A and B to replay their strokes.

4. It's stroke play. After 9 holes Player A hustles into the club-house for a minute. His fellow-competitors, B and C, agree to play from the 10th tee, a par-5 hole, even though it's A's honor. They do and A arrives on the 10th tee just as C plays his stroke. What's the ruling?

_____(a) B and C are both penalized for agreeing to play out of turn.

_____(b) A is penalized for delaying play.

_____(c) B and C have to replay their drives.

_____(d) No penalty.

5. It's a match. A's ball is near the hole but he doesn't mark and lift it. His opponent B putts. B's ball strikes that of A and into the hole goes A's ball. Which is correct?

_____(a) A is considered to have holed out with his previous stroke.

_____(b) No penalty, but A must replace his ball.

_____(c) B is penalized for causing A's ball to move.

_____(d) A is penalized for failing to lift from a position that might have assisted B.

6. It's the same situation, but this time A wants to mark and lift his ball because he feels its position might assist B, who vehemently claims that A has no right to lift, that in match play the player who is away "controls" the opponent's ball. Who was right?

_____(a) Player A.

_____(b) Player B.

7. A player takes relief from a paved cart path. He drops in the correct area, but his dropping method was to stand erect, face the hole and drop over his shoulder. Before he plays a stroke another

153

player reminds him that, under the 1984 Rules, he hasn't used the correct dropping procedure. Which is correct?

_____(a) The player must play the ball as it lies and suffer a one-stroke penalty.

_____(b) The player may rectify his mistake by dropping the ball correctly. No penalty.

_____(c) The player must drop properly and he incurs a one-stroke penalty.

_____(d) There's no penalty, since the player dropped in a right place.

8. Same situation as above, but this time the player plays a stroke after using the old dropping procedure. The mistake is called to his attention *after* he plays the stroke. Does he

_____(a) Lose the hole in match play?

_____(b) Incur a two-stroke penalty in stroke play?

_____(c) Incur a one-stroke penalty in match or stroke play?

_____(d) Retrieve his ball and drop as the Rules now require?

9. A player's ball is plugged in a bunker, one inch in front of his opponent's ball. The player marks and lifts his ball. The opponent blasts and, of course, the player's lie is altered. What does the player do?

_____(a) He places his ball, without plugging it, in the nearest similar lie within two club-lengths.

_____(b) Drops the ball as near as possible to the point where his ball lay before he lifted it.

_____(c) Re-creates the original lie by smoothing the sand and then plugging the ball as it was originally.

_____(d) He replugs the ball within two club-lengths of where it lay, but without restoring the sand at his original position.

10. A player's ball is eminently playable on dry ground within a water hazard on a par-3 hole, but his backswing is severely restricted because there's a pipe running through the hazard behind his ball. Which of the following is correct?

_____(a) There is no relief without penalty.

_____(b) He can invoke the unplayable lie rule and drop in the hazard.

_____(c) He can return to the tee. His next stroke will count as his second.

_____(d) He can drop without penalty away from the obstruction, as per Rule 24, within the hazard.

11. A player's ball comes to rest against a sprinkler head. He drops the ball one club-length from the sprinkler head under Rule 24-2. The ball rolls almost two club-lengths after being dropped, so that it is almost three club-lengths from the sprinkler head. What is the proper procedure for the player?

_____(a) He must re-drop the ball, as it lies more than two club-lengths from the sprinkler head.

_____(b) The ball is in play and he must play it as it lies.

_____(c) He has the option of playing the ball as it lies or re-dropping.

12. A player's ball lies in a lateral water hazard. He wishes to drop the ball 30 yards behind the hazard under penalty of one stroke, keeping the point where the ball last crossed the hazard margin between himself and the hole. By so doing, he would be able to play over some trees blocking his line. May the player so drop?

_____(a) Yes.

_____(b) No.

13. In stroke play, a competitor is playing from just off the green. His fellow-competitor's caddie is attending the flagstick at the competitor's request. The player plays and the ball strikes the flagstick. What is the ruling?

_____(a) The stroke must be replayed without penalty.

_____(b) The ball shall be played as it lies; there is no penalty, because the stroke was played from off the green.

_____(c) The ball shall be played as it lies and the competitor incurs a two-stroke penalty.

_____(d) The fellow-competitor incurs a two-stroke penalty, as his caddie was attending the flagstick, and the competitor replays without penalty.

14. In any situation whereby a player may lift his ball under a Rule, the player may clean the ball before replacing, dropping or placing it.

_____(a) True.

_____(b) False.

15. In stroke play, a competitor's ball is on the green. He putts and his ball strikes the foot of his fellow-competitor's caddie, who was inattentive and was walking across the competitor's line unintentionally. What is the ruling?

_____(a) There is no penalty, and the ball is played as it lies.

_____(b) There is no penalty, and the ball is replaced and re-putted.

155

_____(c) The fellow-competitor incurs a two-stroke penalty, and the ball is played as it lies.

_____(d) The fellow-competitor incurs a two-stroke penalty, and the ball is replaced and reputted.

16. A player, after hitting his second shot, searches for his ball for a minute or two and does not find it. He returns to the spot from which he played his second shot and drops another ball under Rule 27-1. At that point his original ball is found and less than five minutes had passed since search for the original ball began. May the player abandon the dropped ball and continue play with the original ball?

_____(a) Yes.

_____(b) No.

17. A and B play their better ball against C and D in a match. The proper term for such a match is:

_____(a) Best ball.

_____(b) Better-ball of pair.

_____(c) Four-ball.

_____(d) Foursome.

18. In a four-ball match, A's ball is near the hole in a position to serve as a backstop for B, A's partner, who is preparing to putt. May C or D, the opponents, require A to lift his ball before B putts?

_____(a) Yes.

_____(b) No.

19. A player's ball lies in a sandy area through the green. There is a small mound of sand about six inches behind the ball. The player grounds the club only lightly; however, with his backswing he eliminates the small mound of sand. Is there a penalty?

_____(a) Yes.

_____(b) No.

20. A player's ball is on the bank in a water hazard well above the water line. However, it has just rained, and the ball is in a small depression on the bank and the depression contains some rainwater. The player claims that the rainwater is casual water and that he is entitled to drop out of the depression without penalty, dropping in the water hazard, of course. Is the player right?

_____(a) Yes.

_____(b) No.

21. In stroke play, a player, after a search of one minute, assumes his ball (Ball A) is in a water hazard, but there is no reasonable evidence to that effect. He drops another ball (Ball B) behind the hazard under Rule 26-1 and plays it. He then crosses the hazard and finds his original ball on the other side of the hazard in some rough. Less than five minutes has passed since he began search. What is the ruling?

_____(a) The player abandoned Ball A when he played Ball B. He continues with Ball B without penalty other than the penalty under the water hazard Rule.

_____(b) The player must resume play with Ball A. There is no penalty for having played Ball B, as it was an honest error.

_____(c) The player must resume play with Ball A. He incurs a two-stroke penalty for playing Ball B, as Ball B was a wrong ball.

_____(d) The player must resume play with Ball A. He incurs a two-stroke penalty for playing Ball B, as Ball B was played under a wrong Rule.

22. A player addresses the ball and starts his backswing. In the middle of the backswing the ball moves. He continues his swing and hits the ball. Is he penalized because the ball moved?

_____(a) Yes.

_____(b) No.

23. A player lifts his ball on the putting green and tells his opponent that he damaged the ball on the previous shot and is going to substitute another ball. His opponent looks at the ball and disputes the player's claim that it is unfit for play. The player claims he is the sole judge as to whether his ball is unfit for play. Is the player right?

_____(a) Yes.

_____(b) No.

24. A "rub of the green" occurs when a player gets a bad break such as when his ball comes to rest in a divot in the fairway.

_____(a) True.

_____(b) False.

25. A paved cart path is not an obstruction.

_____(a) True.

_____(b) False.

26. A ball is on the fringe of the green. It is overhanging the edge of the green but no part of it is touching the green. Is the ball deemed to be on the green?

_____(a) Yes.

_____(b) No.

27. A putter with a shaft adjustable for length is legal.

_____(a) True.

_____(b) False.

28. In a match, A by mistake starts with fifteen clubs in his bag. He wins the first three holes and, walking to the 4th tee, he discovers his error. What is the ruling?

_____(a) A is disqualified.

_____(b) A loses each hole on which he carried fifteen clubs; thus he is 3 down instead of 3 up at the 4th tee.

_____(c) A incurs a penalty of two holes with the penalty being applied to the state of the match at the time the violation was discovered. Thus, A is 1 up at the 4th tee.

29. A player by mistake plays his ball from a spot which is out of bounds. His opponent claims that A loses the hole for playing a wrong ball. Is the opponent right?

_____(a) Yes.

_____(b) No.

30. A player playing in the rain may not apply resin to the grips of his club to keep his hands from slipping.

_____(a) True.

_____(b) False.

31. A player brushes aside leaves on his line of putt with his cap. Is this legal?

_____(a) Yes.

_____(b) No.

32. Sand is a loose impediment on the putting green but not elsewhere on the course.

_____(a) True.

_____(b) False.

33. A's ball is in a lateral water hazard. He determines the point where the ball last crossed the hazard margin and drops his ball not nearer the hole three club-lengths from the point where it last crossed the margin. Before A plays, B, the opponent, tells A that he (A) should have dropped within two club-lengths. B claims the hole for violation of the lateral-water-hazard relief Rule. A acknowledges that he dropped in a wrong place, but he claims that he may correct his error by lifting his ball and dropping it in a right place without penalty. Who is right?

———(a) A.

———(b) B.

34. A white line defines an area of ground under repair. A ball lies on the white line, but no part of the ball lies over the inside edge of the line. Is the ball considered to be in the ground-under-repair area?

———(a) Yes.

———(b) No.

35. A and B are playing C and D in a match. Each side is playing one ball. The partners strike off alternately from the teeing grounds and thereafter they strike alternately during the play of each hole. Officially, such a match is called a

———(a) Foursome match.

———(b) Four-ball match.

———(c) Scotch foursome match.

———(d) Gangsome.

36. There are only two regulations in the Rules of Golf governing golf balls—one restricts the size of the ball and the other the weight.

———(a) True.

———(b) False.

37. A player begins a round with thirteen clubs. As he did not exercise his right to carry fourteen clubs when he started, he is prohibited from adding another club during the round.

———(a) True.

———(b) False.

38. In a match between A and B, A repairs a spike mark on his line of putt on Hole 4. B says nothing at the time but he begins looking through his Rules book, and after driving off the next tee, B claims Hole 4 on the grounds that the Rules do not allow repair of spike marks on the line of putt. Is B's claim valid?

———(a) Yes.

———(b) No.

39. In stroke play, a competitor tees his ball slightly in front of the tee-markers and plays. A fellow-competitor then calls the competitor's attention to the fact that he teed off from in front of the markers. What is the ruling?

_____(a) The competitor is penalized two strokes and returns to the tee and plays from within the teeing ground.

_____(b) The competitor must count the stroke played, return to the tee and play from within the teeing ground. The next stroke counts as his second.

_____(c) There is no penalty, since the competitor teed off just slightly in front of the markers, and he continues play with the ball played from in front of the markers.

40. A ball lies just outside a bunker. A loose impediment in the bunker interferes with the player's stroke. The player is entitled to remove the loose impediment.

_____(a) True.

_____(b) False.

41. A ball lies in the rough. The player removes a twig that lies about six inches behind the ball. The ball does not move. A few seconds later, as the player is selecting a club, a gust of wind causes the ball to move. The player incurs a penalty.

_____(a) True.

_____(b) False.

42. In match play, a player and his opponent exchange balls during the play of a hole and it cannot be determined who played the wrong ball first. What is the ruling?

_____(a) The hole should be played out with the balls exchanged.

_____(b) Both players should be disqualified.

_____(c) The winner of the hole should be decided by lot.

_____(d) The hole should be considered halved.

43. A player's ball is picked up from the rough by a spectator who thought it was a stray ball. The spectator returns the ball to the player. Under the Rules, the player shall replace the ball on the spot from which it was lifted, but the spectator cannot recall the exact spot. The player drops the ball as near as possible to the spot from which it was lifted. Is the player correct?

_____(a) Yes.

_____(b) No.

44. In match play, a player's ball is behind a tree. He tries to play around the tree but the ball hits the tree, rebounds, hits the player and bounces into an unplayable lie. Is the player penalized because the ball struck him?

_____(a) No. In equity, there is no penalty, because the player did not benefit as a result of the ball having struck him.

_____(b) Yes. The player loses the hole.

_____(c) No, because the player did not purposely allow the ball to strike him.

_____(d) Yes. The player is disqualified.

45. A player addresses his ball on the green. He steps back as a gust of wind comes up. The wind then blows hard and causes the ball to move. No penalty, because he did not cause the ball to move.

_____(a) True.

_____(b) False.

46. A player cuts his ball with a skulled shot on the 4th hole but he does not notice that the ball has been damaged. He drives from the 5th tee and then discovers that the ball had been cut on the previous hole. May the player substitute another ball at that point?

_____(a) Yes.

_____(b) No.

47. A player's drive is hooked into high rough near a boundary. He hits a provisional ball in the fairway nearer the hole than the spot where his original ball presumably came to rest. He looks for the original ball for a minute but does not find it. He moves on to the provisional ball and plays it. At that point, the player's caddie finds the original ball. What is the ruling?

_____(a) The player loses the hole, because he did not search for the original ball for five minutes.

_____(b) The player must abandon the provisional ball and continue play with the original, since he did not search for it for five minutes and therefore it was not lost.

_____(c) The original ball was deemed lost when he played the second shot with the provisional ball; he must continue play with the provisional ball.

48. During a match play competition, bad weather renders the course unplayable. In such a case the Committee has authority to suspend play and resume the matches from the points at which they were discontinued or cancel the round and start all discontinued matches over again.

_____(a) True.

_____(b) False.

49. In stroke play, a competitor returns his score card to the Committee. The hole-by-hole scores are correct; however, the total for one 9 as entered on the card by the competitor is incorrect. What is the penalty, if any?

_____(a) No penalty. The Committee should correct the error.

_____(b) Disqualification.

_____(c) Two strokes. The Committee should correct the error.

50. In a four-ball match, a player putts and his ball strikes his partner's ball and moves it. What is the ruling?

_____(a) The player and his partner lose the hole.

_____(b) No penalty; the partner must replace his ball.

_____(c) No penalty; both balls are played as they lie.

_____(d) No penalty; the partner has the option of playing his ball as it lies or replacing it.

ANSWERS

1. c (R. 7-1)	26. b (R. 16)
2. c (R. 8-1)	27. b (R. 4-1)
3. c (R. 10-1)	28. c (R. 4-4)
4. d (R. 10-2)	29. a (Def. and R. 15)
5. b (R. 18-5)	30. b (R. 14-3)
6. a (R. 22)	31. b (R. 16-1)
7. b (R. 20-6)	32. a (R. 23)
8. c (R. 20-2)	33. a (R. 20-6)
9. c (R. 20-3)	34. a (R. 25)
10. a (R. 24-2)	35. a (R. 29)
11. b (R. 20-2)	36. b (R. 5-1)
12. a (R. 26-1)	37. b (R. 4-4)
13. c (R. 17-3)	38. b (R. 2-5 and R. 34-1)
14. b (R. 21)	39. a (R. 11-3)
15. b (R. 19-1)	40. a (R. 23-1)
16. b (R. 20-4)	41. a (R. 18-2)
17. c (R. 30)	42. a (R. 15-2)
18. a (R. 22)	43. a (R. 20-3)
19. b (R. 13-2)	44. b (R. 19-2)
20. b (R. 25)	45. b (R. 18-2)
21. c (R. 15 and 26-1)	46. b (R. 5-3)
22. a (R. 18-2)	47. c (R. 27-2)
23. b (R. 5-3)	48. b (R. 33-2)
24. b (Def.)	49. a (R. 33-5)
25. b (R. 24)	50. b (R. 18-5 and 19-5)

PRINCIPAL CHANGES SINCE 1983

PRINCIPAL CHANGES SINCE 1983

4-1

Form and Make of Clubs

Previously, flat sides were allowed on all grips. In the new Rules, the grips for all clubs, except putters, are required to be generally circular in cross-section. Flat sides will continue to be allowed in putter grips.

6-3

Time of Starting

The penalty of disqualification for late starting has been retained. However, a Note has been added to provide that a Committee may, in the conditions of a competition, modify the penalty for being up to five minutes late to loss of the first hole to be played in match play or two strokes in stroke play.

7

Practice

Amended to limit practice between holes to putts or chips on or near the putting green of the hole last played, any practice putting green or the next teeing ground. Such practice strokes must not be played from a hazard.

The prohibition against practice on a competition course before a stroke play round has been expanded to prohibit also the testing of the surface of any putting green on the course before such a round.

8-1

Advice

A note has been added permitting the Committee in charge of a team competition to allow each team to receive advice from one person such as a team captain or coach. However, this will not be permissible if an individual competition is being held concurrently with the team competition.

10

Order of Play

In all forms of match play, a player may require his opponent to replay a stroke played out of turn. Previously, in the case of three-ball and four-ball matches, a player could not require an opponent to replay a stroke played out of turn from through the green or in a hazard.

There is no penalty in stroke play for playing out of turn from the teeing ground or elsewhere unless competitors have agreed to play out of turn for the purpose of giving one of them an advantage. Previously, there was a penalty for deliberately playing out of turn from the teeing ground.

There is no penalty if a ball lying in casual water, ground under repair or a burrowing animal hole is accidentally moved during search. Previously, the player was exempt from penalty only if his ball was moved in probing for it.

12-1
Searching for Ball

In all forms of play, if a player's ball at rest is moved by another ball, the moved ball must be replaced and the other ball played as it lies. There is no penalty except that in stroke play, if both balls lay on the putting green prior to the stroke, the player of the stroke would continue to be subject to a penalty of two strokes. Previously, in singles match play, if a player's ball at rest was moved by his opponent's ball, the player had the option of playing his ball as it lay or replacing it.

18
Ball at Rest Moved

Before lifting a ball anywhere on the course which must be replaced, its position must be marked. Previously, the Rules required marking the position of a ball before it was lifted on the putting green, but not elsewhere.

20-1
Lifting

In dropping a ball under a Rule, the player is required to stand erect, hold the ball at shoulder height and arm's length and drop it. There is no restriction on the direction the player faces. If the dropped ball touches the player before or after it strikes the ground, the ball must be re-dropped. If the ball strikes the player's equipment, there is no penalty and the ball must be re-dropped.

20-2a
Dropping

Previously, if the lie of a ball to be placed or replaced was altered, the ball had to be placed in the nearest lie within *two* club-lengths which was most similar to that which it originally occupied. Two club-lengths have been reduced to *one* club-length and, in a bunker, the original lie has to be re-created and the ball placed in that lie.

20-3b
Lie of Ball to Be Placed or Replaced Altered

In all forms of play, an opponent or fellow-competitor is permitted to lift his ball if he considers that it might assist any other player or have any other ball lifted if he considers that it might interfere with his play or assist the play of any other player. Formerly, in singles match play, if an opponent's ball was near the hole and the player considered it might be of assistance to him, the player could require his opponent to leave his ball there.

22
Ball Interfering With or Assisting Play

24-2

Immovable Obstructions

If a ball lies in a water hazard, the player is no longer entitled to relief if his swing or stance is interfered with by an immovable obstruction. On the other hand, if an immovable obstruction on a putting green, such as a sprinkler head, intervenes between a ball on the putting green and the hole, relief is permitted.

Exceptions have been added to the Rules giving relief from from immovable obstructions, casual water, ground under repair and burrowing animal holes to withhold relief if (a) it is clearly unreasonable for the player to play a stroke because of interference by any other condition or (b) interference would occur only through use of an unnecessarily abnormal stance, swing or direction of play.

25-1

Casual Water, Ground Under Repair and Certain Damage to Course

If a ball lies in a water hazard, the player is no longer entitled to relief from a hole made by a burrowing animal, reptile or bird which interferes with his swing or stance.

30 and 31

Four-Ball Competition

In four-ball match play and stroke play one partner may represent the side for all or any part of a match or round. Thus, if a player does not arrive on time, his partner may play alone until the player arrives. The player may join his partner between the play of any two holes, but not during the play of a hole.

INDEX TO THE RULES OF GOLF

C

M

O

175

S

For more information on the Rules of Golf, the following publications are available for purchase from the United States Golf Association:

The Rules of Golf:
as approved by the United States Golf Association. Booklet; $1.00. (Special rates for quantity orders: 50–249, 80¢; 250–999, 65¢; 1,000–9,999, 55¢; 10,000 and up, 40¢.)

The Rules of Golf:
hardcover edition (1984), 6 × 9 inches; $10.00.

Decisions on the Rules of Golf by the United States Golf Association and the Royal and Ancient Golf Club of St. Andrews, Scotland:
interpretations of the Rules of Golf, including the complete Rules and index; hardcover, $25.00.

Golf Rules in Brief:
a four-page pamphlet featuring some basic Rules in easy-to-understand language; 25¢, $10.00 per 100.

How to Behave as a Golfer:
a picture folder on golf course etiquette; 50¢, $15.00 per 100.

Duties of Officials under the Rules of Golf:
contains a checklist of the duties of the referee and other committee members on the course; 50¢.

The Golf Cart and the Rules:
pamphlet; 50¢.

What to Do about Obstructions:
contains useful information on proper procedures under the Rules of Golf pertaining to obstructions; 50¢, $15.00 per 100.

At Sea in a Water Hazard:
a pamphlet on Rules pertaining to water hazards; 50¢, $15.00 per 100.

Prices include shipping by fourth-class mail. Allow four to six weeks for delivery. To order, send checks or money order to:

USGA Publications Order Department
Golf House
Far Hills, New Jersey 07931

New Jersey residents, please add 6% sales tax.
Prices subject to change.

About the Authors

Among **Tom Watson**'s many victories are the U.S. Open in 1982, the Masters in 1977 and 1981, and the British Open in 1975, 1977, 1980, 1982 and 1983. He was the PGA Player of the Year for four consecutive years (five times overall). A graduate of Stanford University, he lives in Mission Hills, Kansas, when he is not touring.

Frank Hannigan is the Senior Executive Director of the United States Golf Association, the governing body of golf in this country. Since 1961 he has helped to conduct nearly 150 USGA championships and international competitions. Hannigan is also widely known as a golf writer, television commentator and producer.